The City Grower

The City Grower

Design, create & manage a small food-growing plot

Matt Franks

Photography by Rachel Warne

KYLE BOOKS

First published in Great Britain in 2016 by
Kyle Books
an imprint of Kyle Cathie Limited
192–198 Vauxhall Bridge Road
London SW1V 1DX
general.enquiries@kylebooks.co.uk
www.kylebooks.co.uk

10 9 8 7 6 5 4 3 2 1

ISBN: 978 0 85783 304 4

A CIP catalogue record for this title is available from the British Library

Editor: Vicky Orchard
Design: Alice Laurent
Photography: Rachel Warne
Illustration: Sam Brewster
Production: Lisa Pinnell

Colour reproduction by F1, London
Printed and bound in China by C&C Offset Printing Co., Ltd

Contents

Introduction

If, like me, you live in a city and want to grow your own food, this book is for you.

Growing your own fruit and vegetables not only means that you eat fresh but that you also help the environment, your own well-being and your wallet.

The fast pace of city life can leave us with little downtime or space to breathe, let alone grow our own food. Whether it's the daily commute or long working hours, even finding the time to fit in a weekly food shop can be a struggle. In this book I will look at ways to juggle a manic workload and enjoy a busy social life while also successfully growing your own produce.

Space is at a premium in urban settings, and many of us don't have a lot of what's available. Over 50 per cent of the world's population now live in cities, and this figure is expected to rise to 66 per cent by 2030 – meaning more competition for this free space. But this shouldn't stop us being able to grow our own food; there are lots of clever ways in which you can grow fresh fruit and vegetables at home, and in spaces that you might have overlooked or thought too small for the purpose.

Another reason why people are interested in growing their own is because they are starting to look at food in a whole new light and want to know where their food has come from. The rise in popularity of veg box schemes and farmers' markets in urban areas shows a steady demand for fresh, seasonal, ethically sourced and organic produce. We are becoming more conscious about the food we eat and are wary of the ills of mass-produced food. This hunger to know more about what we eat has seen us find new and clever ways to grow foods. Having your very own personal growing plot gives you control over the food that you and your friends and family consume and the vitamins and natural goodness you can get from it. And you can't get fresher than your own home-grown produce when it comes just metres from plot to plate!

So if you're looking to eat a healthier diet and want to reconnect with nature, the best way is to get your hands dirty and get growing. It's enlightening, uplifting and invigorating stuff – from the furtive glance in the morning before work through to the moment you see your crops breaking through the surface of the soil and finishing with that fantastic moment when you taste the first home-grown harvest. It will take work, but the endeavour will be its own reward. You don't need to know that much about food growing to produce great crops, you simply need to be able to follow easy instructions and be willing to just pick it up as you go.

With just five simple steps you can design, create and manage your very own small growing space and start enjoying your own food in no time.

I'll be guiding you from proposal to plate. I'll start by drawing up a clear plan of what to do, what to assess and how to get things growing and when. I can help you find the spaces around your home that you may have dismissed as unsuitable for growing crops, which provide the right conditions for your plants.

Armed with tips and gardening aids – available both on- and offline – you can keep your plot healthy without feeling overwhelmed or becoming tied to it. I'll explain how you can upcycle discarded and reclaimed materials to make your planters, give you tips about how to keep pests at bay simply by using commonplace household items or natural methods, and show you when and where to grow certain types of vegetables and fruits. I also look at how you can use handy apps on your smartphone to help yield maximum produce.

To begin, you'll need to create a plot or build a planter to accommodate your crops. I'll show you how to build simply, quickly and effectively to ensure you harvest the best crops in ample supply. Designs can be scalable, too, so that you can adapt them to whatever space you have, be it a full garden or a shaded balcony.

Probably the trickiest part of yielding a healthy harvest is maintenance, but the maintenance programme will ensure the plants work for you. By using a few neat apps on your smartphone the maintenance of your bountiful growing plot can be made to work around your lifestyle. When you create a micro-managed plot you'll be astounded by the produce that you can grow – and keep growing.

I also look at how and when to harvest. For those who have never grown their own before, the taste of your own produce will be a revelation, a money-can't-buy, better-than-farmers'-market sensation that will blow your socks off!

And, most importantly, I'll show you how to grow healthy crops that produce a good yield every year.

Why should we grow food at home even with limited space?

'For me gardening is a such a treat. It connects me with nature when I feel overwhelmed by technology and the fast pace of city life. It also allows me to eat more healthily and easily from home. Nothing tastes as good as your own harvest! So let's get growing...' **Janelle Conn**

'Your planter will serve as a place to relax, to have contact with nature and to get food to add to meals. I have crafted a list of planting plans that provide a rigid approach to gaining plenty of crops with minimum effort. If you want to add new crops or herbs to the planter, go right ahead, it really won't have too much impact on the overall growing process and if it means you visiting more often because you've added a particular crop that you eat all the time, the more the merrier.

'Ideally your planter should become an extension of your kitchen. A place to go to to collect snippets to add to your meals. This plot will add to your palate and educate you and those around you about seasonality and the lifespan of crops, which sometimes I take for granted. I have designed the planting plans to offer something to eat as often as possible, as quickly as possible – there are no crops that take years to come to fruition here. It should hopefully be a fun experiment that turns into an easy and healthy habit.' **Matt Franks**

Before you begin

First off, before you read on, go and stick a bucket or old bin outside where it can collect rainwater (we'll come back to this later…) and then:

→ Start saving toilet roll tubes – these are for planting seedlings.

→ Find your nearest scaffold yard – to source planter materials.

→ Find a local farm/horse riding centre/ friend who lives in the countryside – this will help you source organic matter for plant food and allow you to create rich organic compost.

Plot

In this chapter I'll help you locate the perfect space for your growing plot. It's crucial that you put your plants in the right place for them to grow to their best.

You can grow crops in the most unusual of spaces; it's just about finding the right ones for your plants. Here I will look at how to decide on those ideal spots around your home, some of which you may never have thought about for growing in before. I'll also look at how you can increase the space you have in your plot and make more of it – thinking about the vertical spaces, as well as the horizontal. A plot is available in almost any space if you look for it...

Let there be light!

Finding the right spot generally means finding one with enough light for plants to grow, as light is key to healthy plants. Growing food in any environment, especially an urban one, is about locating a position with enough sunlight and aiming your crops at it. So it's worthwhile taking the time to make adjustments to your plot to increase the exposure to sunlight that it will get.

Living in an urban environment means that you can often be overshadowed by neighbouring properties or high-rise buildings. If this is the case, don't despair, it just means you need to be crafty and more imaginative about how and where you grow – which is part of the fun.

The first thing to do is take out your smartphone, hit maps and orientate the map so that you can see which direction your potential growing plot will be facing. South-facing spaces are best, but west- and east-facing will work too (depending on the level of shade in that part of your garden). North-facing plots aren't as good for growing but there are still lots of crops that will grow in less sunny spaces (see the planting plans in chapter 3).

You can also download a light-meter app on your smartphone that can help here.

There are lots available for iOS and Android. Try Megaman® LuxMeter for iOS (available from the App Store), which is free and good for reading light intensity and coverage, or for Android phones try Lux Meter (also free).

Using these meters is very simple. Just enter the area you want to grow in or that you suspect might have the right growing conditions, and fire up the app.

Simple guidelines for the light levels that you need:

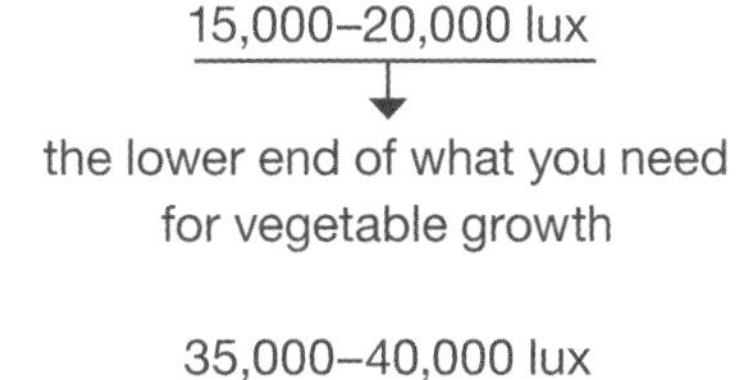

15,000–20,000 lux

the lower end of what you need for vegetable growth

35,000–40,000 lux

what you want to try to hit for flowering crops

These apps can really help when you're trying to find the areas around your home that get the most light. Now you might be thinking, 'why do I need an app for this?', but you just might. The app will allow you to see how broad an area the light covers and at what intensity. It will also get you to think structurally about the space around your home; how you might work with obstacles or structures to give you more space and if possible shift them slightly to increase the light intensity. It's also pretty fun!

After using a lux measurement app you will be able to create a list of a selection of spaces that have sufficient light for growing. Drilling this down to the amount of metres squared you have to grow in will allow you to gauge the amount of food your plot might be able to produce if managed well. This isn't a floor plan of your garden, more a simple list of the best places in which to grow.

These apps can work for both outdoor and indoor growing, although I will only focus on outdoor growing in this book as indoor growing holds many nuanced requirements and would be an entire book in itself!

It takes quite a few hours of sunlight to grow food well. Bigger plants and those that produce large crops, such as tomatoes and

pumpkins, unsurprisingly require the most sunlight. On average you will need about 6 hours of sunlight each day for heavy cropping plants, but in a city it's often hard to get that much, so here I will focus on produce that doesn't require such intensive sun worship. In the next few chapters I concentrate on hardy crops that perform well in imperfect conditions, those that like it a little grey and shaded. However, if you do find you have as much as 6 hours of sunlight a day (because you are lucky or have a raised elevation), I have created a planting plan just for you, too. For those less fortunate, I want to take a look at really evaluating what direct light you have available and how you can capitalise on that.

Reach for the sky!

Finding empty space in a city is tough. Building a productive food plot in a tiny space can also be tough. I want you to grow and produce meaningful amounts of food; food that can be added to each meal that you cook and bring to it new flavours and health properties. For this reason I want you to climb – growing climbing crops allows them to spread out and benefit from natural light. It also makes them easier to water and to reach when it's time to harvest.

One of the benefits of growing vertically is that it allows you to potentially alleviate the problems faced in cities where you need to reach for the light and it helps you to grow lots of produce from only a small area of floor space. If you are aiming to grow vertically, when evaluating your available space see if there are any structures that you can utilise that will allow you to grow upwards and make sure you don't ignore any walls that you might have. You need a clear, high area of wall with no obstacles – such as windows, building projections or air-conditioning vents – and where the plants won't obstruct guttering and wiring. Here's where growing in a city has its benefits!

The chances are you're more likely to be in close proximity to other buildings, so you have more wall climbing options to choose from and the added benefit of shelter from the wind. This can create ideal conditions to grow food, provided you still have enough sunlight. You don't necessarily need to fix attachments to the wall – the side of your home or the neighbour's wall will give you a surface on which you can just lean a number of canes on, or an old set of ladders or even a drainpipe to use as growing support.

The vertical structure you choose should ideally be south-facing and stable – an old shed or fence might not take the weight of the crop you choose to grow. To make this space work for you, think about how your crops grow – are they large plants that tend to lie on the soil or do they like to climb?

(Maybe shoot to Google here to see how big some of the crops you are thinking of growing become.) With this information you can plan the vertical space and position of certain plants so that they don't shade or hinder others. This will give you greater returns for your efforts and not leave wasted space around your plot.

Stealing space

In a city you'll be unlikely to have the absolutely perfect space to grow, so you might have to steal it from the buildings around you. Use the walls of other buildings to prop up your crops; use drainpipes to support climbers; use a fence to offer them shade and think about using existing features like trellis to grow your crops up and along: a picket fence or even an old wine rack will give those climbers something to reach for and will work just perfectly!

If there are no structures that you can locate your growing area near to or lean something against, can you create one? Using old bits of wood and a cheap ball of twine you can create a vertical structure in no time. The plants don't mind what it looks like! There is no set template for making a vertical frame, it just requires common sense and a bit of ingenuity; make the structure wider at the bottom than it is at the top, and making it 3D rather than 2D will create a much more stable platform to support your crops (think pyramids). It doesn't need to be a three-storey monster, something only 1.5m high will work perfectly to give your crops room to grow and allow the air and light to reach right around them. Consider this before you create your plot evaluation, and with this in mind, add in the extra space you will gain.

Pests of the two-legged kind

I've not experienced it much, to be honest, and in reality most people only ever cast praise on your efforts if they are in public view, but there are cases where people can get a little too interested in what you are growing and sample the goods. So be wary of growing near to public paths and other open spaces where passers-by might get tempted to help themselves.

One way to provide some kind of protection for your beloved crops is to put up some netting and/or to harvest regularly, removing the attractive booty before anyone can get their hands on it. I hope this never befalls you, but it's better to be aware so that you can plan accordingly.

Finding the 'sweet spot'

Finding space to grow plants is a common issue, but don't worry, you will have it somewhere. I'd recommend taking this book out to your plot and using it to measure the space – this book is about 25cm in length. You can, of course, just use a tape measure...

Ideally you want to find yourself at least 1m² to grow in (this will be the size of the planter) and you also want space around the planter to be able to move around it to do any maintenance on the plants. Don't be concerned if you need your planter to be sat in a corner, you can use any perceived space limitations to your advantage. As long as you can reach over your planter from one side to the other to tend your crops, it will be easily workable.

You might know the space you have already, so if you do, be sure to note down the height you have available, too.

Take a look at the listed places around your home that you can grow in. This isn't a floor plan of your home, more of a simple list of places to grow. This should cover all of the potential growing spaces outside your home. Don't forget walls too. Don't let this task take more than 10 minutes – if it does it either means you have a huge home (lucky you!) or you need to be more discerning about where you grow.

In all likelihood you'll have a single space in your plot that you will want to use or have a preference for using. For those of you with more space, try to decide which area is the best based on light and situation.

Reducing the plot options down to just one will concentrate your growing and save time. You could grow in several mini plots but your best bet for success is to focus your efforts and your time making one plot work well. One plot done well is better for the crops and your self-esteem; you can always expand next year.

If you do choose to go for more than one plot, consider the space you'll need to move around them. Think about what the area will look like when it is filled with wild foliage and lots of hanging cascading plants everywhere (it will be like this, promise!), then build this into the space you will need overall. Move between your plot/obstacles/walls with your arms comfortably by your sides and see if

you can move around freely – if you don't leave enough space to do this it might feel too tight and you want to avoid knocking against the edges of your planter in case you damage your crops. This is a consideration that you should make when choosing your planter placement: 'If I locate it there will I be able to move around it and reach right over to the rear of it?' If not, I'll be discussing putting wheels onto the planter shortly, which will allow you to move it for ease of access.

Safety

Now I can't have you climbing up and balancing on the edge of your planter to try to reach runner beans that have climbed 4 metres above the soil. I also don't want you struggling with back-breaking pails of water to keep your plants alive. Plan things well and consider exactly how wild your plants might get and the heights that they can reach as they grow. You'll be hugely impressed with such massive foliage but your health insurance provider might not be. Don't pick a plot in a dangerous spot and be conscious that the space you pick will often have a wet floor around it.

Water, water everywhere

I know I'm covering the basics here, but it's worth noting that you should locate your plot in close proximity to a decent supply of water. Not only will it be easier for you to water your plants regularly with less hassle, but it might also save you a lot of arm-ache – especially if you're carrying around large watering cans. It's ideal to have a tap nearby or you could connect up a rainwater collection butt to a nearby drainpipe. This simple approach really works for you when the weather is bad as the butt will refill continually with rainwater. You might want to connect an overflow hose to this so that once the water butt is full the excess water will run off into your plot rather than flow over its sides. This way you save even more water and still have a large reserve to draw on should you need to, and it ensures the water within the butt remains fresh and doesn't become stagnant.

In chapter 2 I will explain how to build a planter that has a built-in capacity to store water and pass it on to the plants when they need it. Conventional watering often loses a lot of water as run-off, but this design allows you to harvest rainwater within the planter and will provide you with a 'mini-break, fail-safe' approach to watering should you need to be away from your plants for a period of time, and you won't have to worry about them not being watered.

Watering regularly is the one area of growing that many people, myself included, seem to struggle with, as it requires diligence and constant supervision. To grow 1kg of potatoes requires approximately 287 litres

of water – that is three bathfuls of water and then some! Regular watering is worth the effort, though, and it will likely make the difference between a successful crop and trying to harvest from the Gobi Desert. If you want a healthy plot that gives you lots of tasty greens you've got to put the effort in, and in hot, dry weather in particular you'll very likely need to water your plants daily. (Taking this into consideration, there's more about clever ways to collect water later, in chapter 5.)

Rainwater is king. It has fewer mineral elements, and is packed with nutrients your crops will love and actually NEED, so it's best to collect rainwater and use it to water your plot. However, getting hold of enough rainwater can be tough: it really doesn't

Rainwater is king

There are minerals in rainwater that don't exist in tap water (and vice versa) and that are good and bad for plants. Here is what you need to know:

↓

Tap water is 'cleaned' for obvious reasons. This means that it can often include chemicals like chlorine, which kills bacteria. The sign of a healthy plot is an abundance of microorganisms. Rainwater never has chlorine in it.

↓

Tap water also has minerals like magnesium and calcium in it. Plants need magnesium to photosynthesise and most tend to thrive on calcium.

↓

Tap water tends to be neutral pH or slightly alkaline, but plants prefer a slightly acidic water – rainwater gains acidity when it collects carbon dioxide as it falls from the clouds.

↓

Air is mostly nitrogen, so nitrogenous compounds tend to form in rainwater; plants love nitrogen and use it to fuel leaf growth; tap water does not normally have nitrogen in it.

↓

Rainwater tends to have plenty of oxygen in it, tap water has less (which is why plants love the natural stuff), so even with a deluge their roots aren't suffocated because there is so much oxygen in the water!

rain as much as you might think (but this depends where you are in the world!), plus your plants often need more than the weather provides. If you can't build the planter in chapter 2, collect rainwater in a water butt that is connected to guttering as a backup.

Drainage

The flip side of watering is having good drainage – you don't want soil to become mouldy and smelly or for the roots of plants to rot in overly wet conditions. If you are reading this book and choose to grow indoors this needs to be of particular note! Letting the soil dry to the point where your plants just start to wilt and then watering will ensure that you are providing the right amount of water. Outdoor growing will result in water spillage, and you need to consider this and plan for it. The planter design that we'll give you later on in the book makes every effort to conserve this precious resource but even this has its limits. But don't worry, it's not going to be a deluge! You simply need to consider where this water will run and it's ideal if it doesn't pool towards or in your home! To avert this either locate the planter you make on slightly sloping ground or raise up the planter on one side to allow the run-off to fall away from where you live.

Meals on wheels

Buildings can often get in the way of urban growing environments. You can't move these, so there's not much you can do about them, but you can move the plants around to avoid being in their shadow. By adding wheels to the bottom of your planter you can optimise your growing situation. For instance, as the arc of the sun gets higher in the sky through the summer, your access to light might change.

It's unlikely that you'll be able to easily move a large planter once all the compost and soil has become sodden and heavy, unless you put it on wheels. (Moving the planter allows you to be flexible in less than perfect situations and work with the light, which will help you to produce monster crops. More on this in chapter 2.) So if your planter is in a fixed position and can't be moved, you need to pick a location where the plants will be happy and the planter won't cause a nuisance.

Rooftop plots

If you are struggling with space and living in an urban environment, it's likely you'll have a flat roof nearby. If it is on the top of your building, or a friend's building, this could be the answer you are looking for. Flat roofs will be built with more than enough strength to take sitting water, so putting a few plants in pots on it should be no bother at all. Just make sure you ask the owner of the building nicely, if it's not you, and check that the roof can take the load of several pots or a planter. One way you can assess this is to check what the roof is made of; corrugated iron and clay tiles are probably not strong enough, a large slab of concrete will be. If in doubt, ask the owner, and if you're still in doubt, don't take the risk.

Getting up to rooftops and moving around them might be tricky, though, so be careful and make the greatest efforts to stay safe when up there. Don't create plots that are very close to rooftop edges unless they have a wall or railings surrounding them and always take the plot development into consideration – don't add several beds all at once, unless you know the load capacity of the roof. Build one or two first and assess how the roof is coping with this additional weight.

Rooftop growing in a city makes sense: you get great exposure to the sun and you don't have to compromise with neighbours (hopefully...). Take a trip to the top of a high building in any city and you'll see an abundance of under-utilised space. Rooftop planting has another advantage, in that it enables you to produce significant crop numbers from a small space because you can grow vertically, meaning that you don't have to spread yourself about the roof and

can focus on a small area – so you'll save time and energy. Of course rooftop growing can be windy, but you'll be surprised at how much of a battering by wind plants can tolerate. To reduce the impact of the heavens blowing your plants to pieces you should consider adding small windbreaks to the side the wind usually blows from, for instance in the UK winds usually blow up from the south east. To assess this, consult the digital world for guidance and see if there is any seasonality to the winds in your area. This may mean you need to adjust your plant protection through the growing window so could be crucial to success! The windbreaks can be made from anything from card to sheets of plastic. Simply make use of items, such as polythene or packaging box material, you find when you are sourcing

planter materials and make a small 'wall' supported with canes and weighed down with stones or anything else heavy you can find, like old bricks, or tuck it deep into the soil. Added support for your delicate crops can come from planting hardy herbs along one side of your plot and then planting your easily damaged peas and beans behind, safe from all but the hardest of gusts. Either way, rooftop growing is great for access to sun but just consider how to protect your plants from the start or all your hard work could be destroyed.

You can also grow crops that help shade each other (I cover crops that grow well in shade in chapter 3), because although rooftops are good space solutions, you need to be careful your plot doesn't suffer from too much sunlight exposure. Roof growing requires you to reappraise how you consider the sun. You're no longer looking for it but in high summer you will be attempting to hide from it. A way to keep your plants shaded so they don't suffer is to plant in a box formation of vertically growing crops. As the sun moves across the sky, growing in a square formation will allow your crops to only have so much exposure to the sun. The focus for the side that faces south will be sun-loving crops, such as tomatoes. The expanse of foliage will ideally shade the other crops and reduce the watering you need to do.

However, at the exposure level, regular watering will be crucial to keeping everything alive. It's essential you have a tap on the roof and seriously consider installing a simple timed watering system to save you time. This can be bought online from many places (a certain world-famous auction website comes highly recommended…). This will fit to any standard tap and should be bought with a length of hose and drip plugs that are easily applied to the bed you are growing in.

The timing of when and how often is best to water very much depends on where you are in the world and the crops you are growing. It is often a case of experimenting initially to find the ideal setting. It's a good idea to overcompensate at first otherwise your over-reliance on the system may be your downfall; set the timer with a greater frequency than you initially anticipate being necessary and reduce accordingly. You will know you are overwatering if there is considerable run-off from your planter; if so, reduce it back from this point until the run-off is minimal. My advice: in a temperate climate with summer maximum temperature of about 30–33°C you are likely going to need to have three waterings per day for 20 minutes. You are almost forced into this approach due to the rooftop growing conditions – so take the measures necessary to keep your crops healthy.

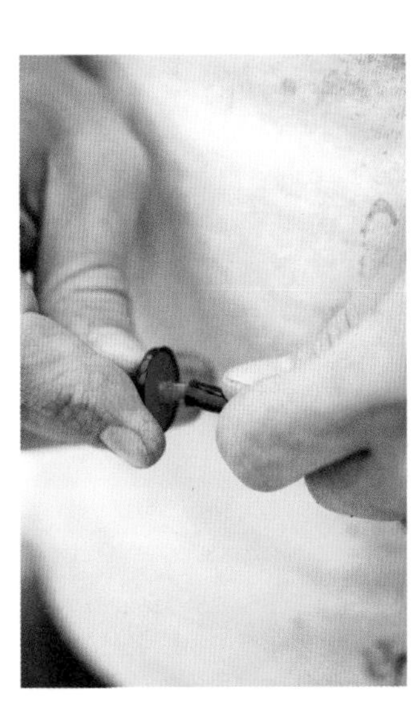

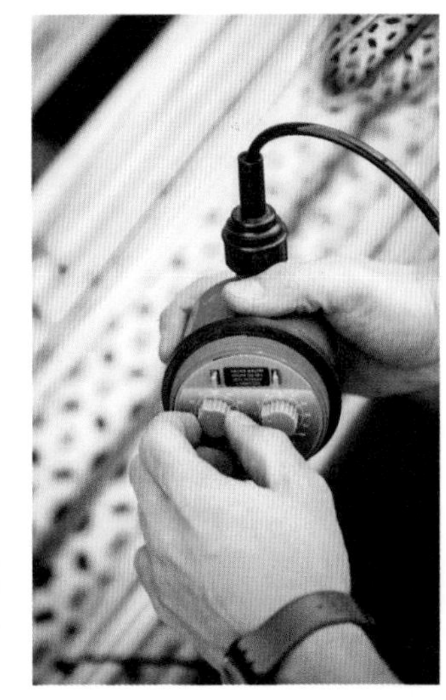

My approach to stress-free, quick water collection:

Firstly, identify an elevated structure against which you can lean a rainwater collector.

Find four lengths of wood, each about 2m long – and a large sheet of polythene. Cut two of them in half, so you now have 2x2m and 4x1m in total.

Make a rectangular frame, using the 2m lengths of wood for the longer sides and two of the 1m lengths for the shorter sides. Screw or hammer them together to create a frame.

Now take the remaining two 1m lengths of wood and lay them on your newly built frame, dividing it into three equal parts (see the bottom left image for reference). Screw or hammer these into place.

Take your frame and rest it against your identified elevated structure at a 45° angle. Lay the polythene over the frame and push it through the gaps in the frame to create water catchment pockets (see images below).

Make the pockets roughly 20-30cm deep, so they will collect rainwater. Once you're happy with the size and depth of your pockets, staple or tack the polythene to the wooden frame.

You now have several water collection pockets that will allow water to pool and once one pocket is filled it will overflow to the one below. This construction doesn't look very pretty but it will do the job perfectly.

After you've collected enough rainwater, get a bucket or watering can, dip it in the collected pools of water and start drenching those plants with the good stuff!

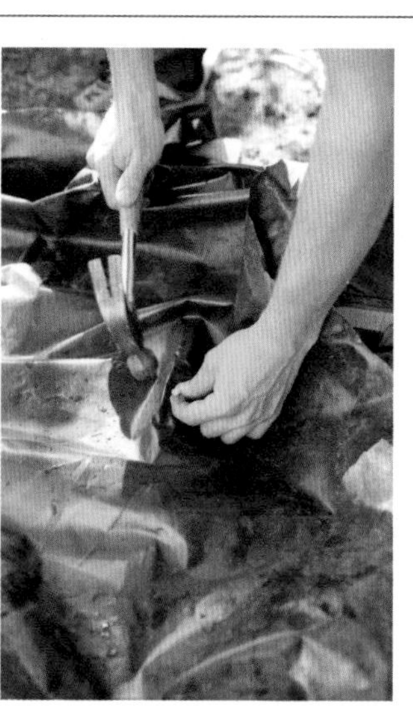

The L.A.W.

My acronym of choice to summarise the key points in the Plot chapter is:

L.A.W. = Light, Access and Water. Follow these three guiding principles and you'll find you will be able to grow bumper crops at home.

Essentials of plot assessment

- You're ideally looking for 1m² of space with 2 metres of height.
- You need direct sunlight for at least 4–6 hours per day.
- You need regular access to water.
- Try to find a wall to grow against; it will increase the potential of your plot.
- Make sure you can move around your plot and you can reach from one side of a planter to the other.

You now know how to...

Tick these things off as you complete them:

- ☐ Know how to find the right plot to grow in (and have found it!).
- ☐ Evaluate how much sunlight your growing plot is getting.
- ☐ Measure the space you have available.
- ☐ Take into consideration growing for the long term.
- ☐ Know how you're going to water your plants.

Extra help

→ On the Connected Roots website we have at least five Vine videos showing the plot-finding process. (Search 'Connected Roots Vine' to find out more or look at www.connectedroots.co.uk)

→ We are constantly building our collection of marvellous urban plots (the places in which people grow always astound us), so if you are uploading, tag yours with #urbanfoodplot on Instagram.

→ I've created lots of inspiration plots on Pinterest for you to marvel at (see page 138).

→ I have created several YouTube videos of the plot pointers I've detailed above. If you fancy seeing this advice in action, watch the short plot summary videos (see page 138).

Taking a steady, considered approach to plot set-up will give you better, healthier crops. A good plot is one that fits into your lifestyle; one that you don't need to spend too much time maintaining.

Build

So you've found the right place for your plot, now it's time to build your planter. Here I give simple build solutions that allow you to create your own growing plot quickly and cost effectively.

This planter is specifically designed for urban environments that may have little or no ground-level soil to plant in and may not have direct access to water. In these situations it is best to construct a raised bed planter.

Raised bed design

Growing in a raised bed planter means that you have tighter control over your growing conditions. By raising your plants up you can effectively combat pests and you save yourself from bending down to dig or do general maintenance, which I am very thankful for! A raised bed planter also gives you the root depth you need to grow healthy crops, with minimal fuss.

Because the planters are elevated they are 'no-dig', meaning you won't need heavy tools or lots of labour to turn over the soil. This 'no-dig' approach also significantly reduces the numbers of weeds you are likely to get – disturbance (the turning over) of soil is what helps to germinate weeds. So by employing the no-dig method you'll not only get fewer weeds and less arm ache, but you also avoid disturbing the microorganisms that exist in the organic matter you have filled the planter with. This promotes healthy soil and, thus, healthy plants.

Growing in a raised bed planter also restricts the space you have – but in a good way. It means you can focus your attention and effort on a smaller number of crops, which is beneficial for beginners and those of us who live in a city and have significant time constraints.

Your build

Nobody enjoys following lots of complex instructions. Let's face it, IKEA flat-packs can test the patience of the best of us. So I'm going to give you a foolproof set of guidelines to create a planter that is very much your own creation.

That said, it does help to think from the perspective of the plants when designing your raised bed planter:
- Do they have enough space?
- Is it deep enough for their roots?
- Will they get enough water?

You don't need to create a work of art; it doesn't have to have smooth, perfect edges, it just has to be something that works for you and gives you the best access to the produce you want to grow.

This planting technique uses good organic matter – it gives the plants the best start possible. By controlling the growing medium, you know what your plant will be drawing out of the earth. This is important because it gives peace of mind, as you never know, in a city, what chemicals might be in the ground or what the area you live in was once used for.

Your newly built planter will be lined with a water-permeable membrane, and this, along with all the organic matter you put inside it, ensures that the plants and soil will stay there and not just fall down into the water reservoir below.

Note: It's important to locate the planter in the place you want it before you start filling it with soil, organic matter and plants and watering it as it will become VERY heavy once filled. If you have chosen to add wheels to the planter this will help significantly here.

Upcycle your planter

I'm a firm advocate of upcycling and trying to repurpose salvage materials for our plots and gardens – I keep my eyes peeled at all times for discarded gardening gems! I've tailored this build guide to allow for using recycled materials so you can keep material costs down and also make your planter unique.

Searching through skips, pillaging discarded building refuse and scanning through restaurant waste might seem radical but it can save you a fortune on materials you need for your planter. Here are a few ideas for where you can go, both on- and offline, to find free or cheap items that you can upcycle/salvage for your plot:

→ Check if your local council offers free compost and where you can obtain it.
→ Visit your nearest recycling depot – this might seem a bit daunting but it can be a great source for larger materials. You don't need permission for this and obviously you're simply helping them to recycle their waste so should be welcome – but ask first before you go plundering through heaps of rubbish.
→ Skips – one man's waste is another man's gold. Think of the large pieces of timber that are often thrown out and how you might use these. You want solid lengths of wood for this planter, but if you spot anything else you think you can use, brilliant!
→ Commercial waste from building sites – namely pallets and other construction materials like timber, old guttering and material you can use for a liner.
→ Scaffold yards are a great source for scaffold boards and wood.
→ Keep your peepers peeled on the city streets – it's increasingly common to see thrown-away items such as pallets left on the street. I recommend always checking that items you find have actually been discarded before taking them, though.

→ Try gumtree.com for local items and materials that might be of use for your build.
→ Join a group on Freecycle online in your area to get free local items and materials.
→ On the online site Preloved.com you can buy second-hand items and materials locally, fairly inexpensively.

Tools and materials
Here I've listed a selection of tools and materials that are fundamental for most planter builds. If you don't have your own tools and don't want to buy them, don't let that stop you. The build won't take too long so if you know anyone with tools you can always borrow them or hire them over a weekend.

→ Saw
→ Hammer
→ A handful of nails
→ A handful of tacks or a staple gun
→ Pencil
→ Chalk
→ Tape measure
→ An old cotton rag or piece of cotton clothing you no longer want
→ Drill and screws (optional)
→ Weed control ground cover membrane – a porous membrane that allows water to leak through but will hold your organic matter in place
→ 2x2m² plastic sheeting. Damp proof membrane (DPM) is perfect here but any other plastic sheeting will do. Available from any DIY store.
→ Scissors or a sharp knife
→ Wooden packaging pallet (pick one that fits your plot size or your preference)
→ 4 x scaffold boards OR 1m long pieces of wood (to fit your pallet, so get that first!)

Wooden packaging pallet

Materials task 1: Source 1 wooden packaging pallet

I recommend using these as the base for your raised bed planter. Wooden pallets are quite easy to find in cities and are often seen discarded on the pavements and roadsides outside restaurants, builders' yards, garden centres and manufacturing companies. If you do have trouble spotting one you can always seek out households currently undergoing refurbishment work or new construction as there pallets will often be in abundance and surplus to requirements. Always ask the homeowner or builder first before helping yourself.

When choosing/finding your pallet, try to get one that looks structurally sound. Are any slats broken or missing? Does it hold together well? You want one that will take the load that you're going to ask it to carry, not one that will collapse when you get it home. Look for a pallet that's fairly light (they can be damn heavy) and is about 1m^2.

Remember, as long as it isn't structurally damaged, it doesn't matter what your pallet looks like, it is only there to provide the base to your planter and it won't be visible in the finished raised bed design.

Scaffold boards

Materials task 2: Source 4 x 1m scaffold boards

Scaffold boards are strong, thick and resilient, yet brilliantly cheap, too. They form the outer skeletons of construction projects the world over and are a commonplace staple on building sites, but – and here is a secret – they must be replaced quite frequently for health and safety reasons, even when there is often nothing wrong with them! This means you are likely to find lots of surplus boards to use. If you can't find them in skips, contact a scaffold yard, as they often sell old boards pretty cheaply.

Scaffold boards are a great addition if you can get them as they'll last for many years but any wooden boards that fit the length of your pallet will work. Pallet sizes can vary considerably, but you are usually looking at about 110 x 75cm – so find timber lengths that meet these requirements.

Note: The list of materials specifies 'nails' as the main construction ingredient. I've gone with nails instead of screws because not everyone has a drill, but if you do or you can find one to borrow, use screws instead because it'll be much easier to adjust the boards in the future should you want to.

Now you've sourced the large materials it's time to roll up your sleeves and start building your planter.

Large planter build

It shouldn't take too long to build your planter; you should be able to construct a $1m^2$ planter in just 30 minutes.

Follow these 10 simple steps to create your very own large raised bed planter. I've also created a video for you to follow should you want any further help – just take a look at the Connected Roots YouTube channel.

→ Take the plastic sheet/DPM and spread it out on the ground outside. Ideally do this where you are going to locate your planter but this isn't essential.

→ Place the pallet on top of the plastic sheet/DPM.

→ Using a tape measure and ruler, mark out 15cm from all the edges of the pallet on the plastic sheet/DPM in chalk. It should look like you have framed the pallet when seen from above.

→ Using scissors or a sharp knife, cut the plastic sheet/DPM along the chalk marks so that you have left an extra 15cm of plastic sheeting/DPM around all sides of the pallet.

→ Next, cut out the four corners of the plastic sheet/DPM.

→ Bring the plastic sheet/DPM up the outer sides of the pallet and either staple or tack it into place. Make sure the plastic sheet/DPM is taut on all sides.

→ Take a scaffold board and cut it to the length of one side of the pallet with a saw or power tool, if you have one. It doesn't have to look perfect and, in all honesty, if your

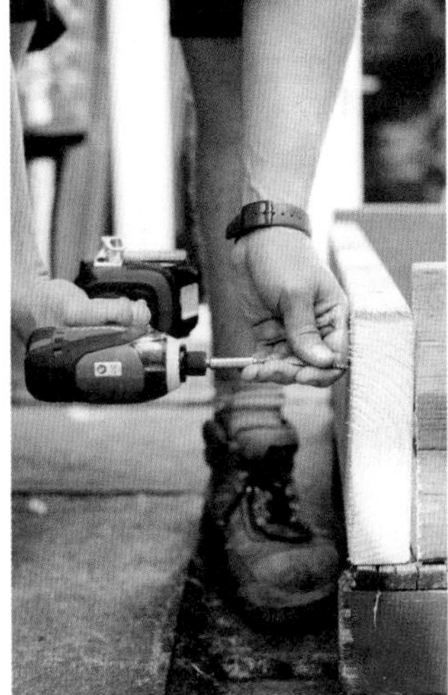

boards are roughly the right length anyway just let them hang over the ends of the pallet.

→ Repeat this three more times to create the first level of the side of your planter. Fit the boards together at the corners and nail/screw them together and to the pallet.

→ Repeat once more to add height to the sides of the planter. Try to vary where the boards overlap at the corners from the first set of scaffold boards for additional structural rigidity.

→ Use a water-permeable liner such as the weed control membrane to line the void of the planter and secure it with a staple gun, if you have one, or just use some tacks.

Note

You can paint the planter on the outside if you want to. Try to stop a few centimetres from the top of the planter so that the plants don't come into contact with the paint; you don't want any potentially nasty chemicals going near your crops.

Wheelie good plants

Surrounding buildings and poor access to prolonged daylight mean that urban growing can be difficult (see chapter 1). One of the main problems you might face is not having enough sun. You could get around this by shifting your planter to follow the sun. Another issue may be watering, if you have to carry water over long distances to reach

your plants. This can be time consuming and a lot of effort lugging heavy watering cans around. The solution could be adding wheels to your planter, which will help with both of these problems.

Now, you can't really 'find' caster wheels in skips or suchlike. You might stumble across them but there isn't a guaranteed place where they exist in large numbers for free, so your best bet is to buy them online or from a local DIY or hardware store. They are available for the price of a couple of cups of coffee and will save you a lot of backache, so they are worth it. To extend your construction to this level requires a drill to fit the wheels to the underside of the planter – don't try this with nails!

Fitting

This will take 2–3 minutes to do and will give extra scope and versatility to your planter.

Lay the planter on its side to create a stable planter and ease of access. Make sure you get at least two swivel wheels when you buy them otherwise the finished planter will only go in one direction – not ideal! Screw the two swivel wheels on one side (see photos), attach the remaining wheels and then you're done!

It might be an idea to fit one wheel with a brake if you are locating the planter on an uneven surface, to ensure it doesn't slide around dangerously! If you need to do this, you can usually buy a caster wheel with a brake as a single unit. This wheel is no different to the other caster wheels and simply needs screwing into place just like the others.

Small planter build

You might not have the space for a large planter, or your space might require you to grow in a shallower form, so you might prefer to make a smaller planter. The raised bed planter guide is scalable, so you can create a smaller version to fit into tighter spaces.

To create a smaller planter you will need to use a smaller base pallet. You can get quite small pallets that are about 90 x 70cm, so see if this will fit your space. If you can't find one that fits these rough dimensions simply cut down a larger pallet. It's a bit more effort but it will work just as well.

You will also need smaller scaffold boards – roughly 90cm x 70cm. You may only need offcuts, though, so it's worth asking a scaffold yard if there are any that you can collect for free.

Follow these 10 simple steps to create your very own small raised bed planter:

→ Take the plastic sheet/DPM and spread it out on the ground. Again, as with the larger planter, it saves time and effort if you do this task where you will finally locate the finished planter.
→ Place the pallet on top of the plastic sheet/DPM.
→ Using a tape measure and ruler, mark out 10cm around the edges of the pallet on the plastic sheet/DPM in chalk.

→ Using scissors or a sharp knife, cut the plastic sheet/DPM along the chalk marks so you have an extra 10cm of plastic sheeting/ DPM around all sides of the pallet. It should look like you have framed the pallet when seen from above.

→ Next, cut out the corners of the plastic sheet, as for the larger planter.

→ Bring the plastic sheet/DPM up the outer sides of the pallet and either staple or tack it into place. Make sure the plastic sheet/DPM is taut on all sides.

→ Take a scaffold board and cut it to the length of one side of the pallet with a saw. It doesn't have to look perfect and in all honesty, if your boards are roughly the right length to fit the pallet then just let them hang over the ends of the pallet.

→ Repeat this three more times to create the first level of the side of your planter. Fit the boards together at the corners so you can screw them together. Now screw them to the pallet.

→ Repeat once more to add height to the sides of the planter. Try to vary where the boards overlap at the corners from the first set of scaffold boards for additional structural rigidity.

→ Use a liner, such as the weed control membrane, to line the void of the planter and secure it with a staple gun, if you have one, or just use some tacks.

Good effort so far!

You've created a self-irrigating, sustainable urban garden for almost no cost. The reason for wrapping the pallet in the plastic sheeting is so that this part of the planter will collect water, both tap water and rainwater. You've created a reservoir at the base of the planter but you've also created an overflow mechanism so that older water is replaced at each watering so that it doesn't become stagnant. As fresh water is continually added to the reservoir and water leaves the planter by the overflow it will prevent stagnation. The cotton rag you have sourced will be used to create a capillary action once installed, to draw the water from the reservoir to the plant roots. Plants only draw water when they need it and so can never be overwatered if you use this technique.

Working with the space you have – other options

This planter design is one that anyone can construct very quickly to create a home growing plot. But not everyone will have the time or the space to accommodate and build a planter, so see pages 52–55 for other, even quicker, solutions to home growing planters. It's all about how resourceful (and sometimes how cheeky) you are prepared to be to find something to grow in!

Tyre stack planter

Materials task 3: If you're not going down the pallet route, get 4 tyres and roll them home.

Make friends with your local tyre workshop or garage and it will develop into a wonderful symbiotic relationship with used tyres as the currency. You see (here's another little secret), garages often have to pay to get rid of used tyres, because there is a government-imposed tax to deal with the sheer number of tyres that end up in landfill. This situation might change depending on where you are in the world, but the simple fact remains that a huge amount of tyres are changed and discarded each year, and to be able to help recycle them can only be a good thing.

Tyres are a ready-made plug-and-grow planter. The workshop or garage will be happy for you to help them reduce their surplus, so don't be worried about asking. Simply whack them in the spot you want them to grow in, then skip forward to Chapter 4 and the lasagne compost to get growing (see page 91). You don't need to line them, you don't need to puncture them to let the water out and you don't need to bind them together. It's about as simple as you can get.

You can make the tyre planter as deep or as shallow as you want.

These stacks are great for growing strawberries and potatoes, as the berries need to hang down and potatoes, being root vegetables, like to go deep. You can even stack up more tyres as you need them. They're great for most things – so go and find some old rubber and get growing in seconds. (See our Pinterest page/board for tyre planter solutions.)

Oil drum planter

Materials task 4:
If a pallet is too big for your growing space or you want to mix things up, get 2–3 large, empty oil drums.

Restaurants and eateries, especially larger ones, use industrial drums of cooking oils. They seem to go through these quickly and often have lots to throw away. If you go and ask, they might allow you to have the old ones. And, wonderfully, these drums are usually brightly coloured and designed with eye-catching appeal so they make an attractive as well as practical addition to any garden, big or small.

Oil drums make a quick and easy ready-made planter. If you don't feel like going in and asking, many restaurants will normally just sit these by the roadside on rubbish collection day, so you can nip out and take them then.

If you can, take more than you need and then post what you don't want on our Facebook page or tweet us @connectedroots so that others can find out where to get them from too. We'll retweet your message to our followers and hopefully others will seek you out.

The only thing you need to do with the oil drum is cut the top off. Dependent on the lip of the drum, you might be able to use a can opener. I've found that the best way to do this is with an old chisel that pierces the tin. Be very careful when removing the lid and try to get some help, as this will be like opening a large can of beans and it will have seriously sharp edges. Maybe wear gloves to do this to save having to visit a doctor!

Once you've removed the top of the drum, be sure to bend the edge of the lip inwards towards the side of the tin to ensure that you or others don't injure themselves on the sharp edge. Do this with a hammer or a pair of pliers. Be careful how you convert your oil drum and make sure it's safe, with any remaining sharp edges hammered down flat against the sides of the drum before you start planting in it.

Constructing your planter should be fun and shouldn't take all day. If it gets too laborious, you're investing too much time in the job. Just remember the whole time you're doing it that your plants will be happy with some healthy organic matter and some nutritious water and feed. It's not really about the vessel they are contained within – as long as it holds together and the plants have enough organic matter to root around in, all will be well. I've given you some ideas and a structure about what you can build but each country will vary in what surplus materials it has lying around – in Australia and New Zealand, for instance, fruit pallets abound! Use whatever you can find that looks fit for purpose and get growing.

Above all, Keep It Simple, Stupid – KISS!

Plan

Now you've made your planter – imaginatively sourced and at minimal cost – and it's positioned in the right spot, you have your growing space sorted. But before you start planting your seedlings you need to plan what you want to grow and when.

We've all been there; you get lots of seeds you fancy growing, but you don't really know when you need to plant them, where to plant them or how to plant them, so you just stick them in some soil, water them and hope for the best. If you don't have success you can end up feeling like you don't know where to start and confused as to why things aren't growing.

Some plants grow really well together, others don't. Some crops will need other plants to give them shelter and support to grow to their best, others prefer to have plenty of room and to be left alone to get on with it.

Trying to grow crops en masse, in uniform rows, is unnatural and does not deliver the supportive ecosystem that all plants need.

I want you to create a diverse, eclectic, natural wonderland, a pocket of wildlife in an urban sprawl and one that will provide rich tastes, bold colours and textures.

In this chapter I will explain, simply and effectively, how to plant a successful crop from the off. There are also planting plans that will generate lots of food of different kinds, tastes, shapes and sizes, and I'll provide lots of hands-on advice through social media so that you can watch, listen and query to your heart's content.

Planting plans

If you follow this simple planting plan you'll be surprised at how easy growing your own food can be. I use several scalable plans that feature plants that work perfectly together, as nature intended – such as basil and tomatoes, and carrot and coriander. What works in the kitchen also works in the garden! I will be giving clear guidance on the best crops that deliver high yields in a short space of time and which also help their companion crops to flourish.

Our planting plans allow you to produce more food because instead of growing one crop, you grow several at different heights, each of which provide symbiotic benefits to the others. The way I, and now you, grow will mean less watering, no digging, very few weeds and most importantly no chemicals.

In some urban environments there are going to be light and space limitations, so we have outlined a shade-specific planting plan, and one that copes well with little attention, for those of you for whom time is a rare commodity. The standard planter I recommend building in the previous chapter will also help here, too.

Before you get started ordering seeds, think about which foods you want to grow, what you love the taste of, or perhaps don't buy too often in the shops as it's quite expensive. Make a list and see if you can come up with your own planting plan, or failing that, use the planting plans I have devloped and edit them to your heart's content. The important thing here is to grow what you love to eat!

Our plans include an eclectic selection of crops, and foods that are healthy and that taste good. The fruit and vegetables that you pick from your own growing plot will always be fresher and taste better than those you buy in the supermarket, which have been flown from the other side of the world and sprayed with a dozen chemical pesticides and fungicides to keep them 'fresh'.

The basics

It is essential that before you start to create your planting plan you have guidance on the catch-all terms that we will mention within the plans themselves. This will give you an understanding of the plants you might choose to grow and will hopefully whet your appetite.

I don't want to bog you down with lots of horticultural jargon, but there are a few key terms that are worth being familiar with, as they will crop up regularly:

Annual
An annual plant is one that germinates, flowers and dies (or is harvested before it dies) all in one year.

Biennial
A biennial plant takes two years to complete its life cycle.

Perennial
A perennial plant is one that lives for more than two years.

Cut-and-come-again
Some vegetables, such as lettuces, do not have to be grown to full maturity. Instead, you can harvest their leaves by cutting or

picking them as and when you need them, after which the plant will keep growing to give you further harvests. The main advantages to cropping them this way are that it avoids gluts, makes harvesting mixed leaves in usable quantities easier and you can get a longer, steadier harvest from a small space.

Running to seed/bolting
This is when a plant begins to try to form seeds, and is usually accompanied by rapid formation of flowers. It is generally triggered by a cold spell, or by changes in day length, or by an extended dry period.

Sowing direct
This is when you sow seeds straight into the soil of your planter rather than start them off in seed trays, etc., and transfer them when they are larger.

Sowing under cover
Some seeds are better sown on a windowsill, or under a 'cloche' such as an old plastic container rather than outdoors, in order to protect them from pests and/or provide more warmth.

Urban propagation
This means growing plants from seeds to seedlings in egg boxes/yogurt pots/jam jar/old shoes/ANYTHING on windowsills. You can grow your seeds in any container you can lay your hands on and just pop them on any sunny windowsill or shelf you can find. It doesn't have to be fancy, it just needs to hold enough soil for the little seed to germinate and you'll be away! You don't need an expensive greenhouse or polytunnel to be a grower! We'd love to see how you get on with this and how inventive you can be, so do share photos with us at Connected Roots through the usual social media channels (see page 138).

Picking your plants

Now we'll cover some key plants that form the bedrock of the urban food plot and also look at your herb-growing set-up.

Tender herbs

These tend to be annual herbs such as chives, basil and coriander – as annuals (see page 60) they normally last only one year but they can self-seed, so you might have some seedlings popping up the next year where they grew the year before. They also tend to not like very cold weather, so they will generally be finished outdoors by the time the first frosts come around.

Woody herbs

These are usually perennial plants (see page 60) such as rosemary, thyme and sage, and if looked after well with no diseases these herbs can last for years. They are normally resistant to very cold weather but if temperatures are predicted to drop down as far as -20°C, be sure to wrap them (and probably everything else in your planter!) in horticultural fleece, bubble wrap or an old jumper (!), or bring them indoors to make sure they don't die.

Good herbs to grow

Annuals (generally tender)
Basil, leaf celery, dill, parsley, coriander.

Perennials (generally quite hardy)
Rosemary, sage, thyme, lemon balm, oregano, mint, chives, lovage, Echinacea, summer and winter savory, chamomile.

Salad plants

Perpetual spinach – also known as leaf beet, this vegetable is a member of the beetroot family but is grown for its green leaves. It tastes similar to spinach, hence the name, but it tends not to go to seed, is perennial and is much more acclimatised to cold weather.
Curly kale – delicious perennial brassica (plants from the cabbage family) that is happy in cold weather and generally does not go to seed too easily.

Oriental greens – Asian leaves are the perfect crop for a small plot. They are fast growing, don't need a lot of sun, and can be eaten in either salads or stir-fries. Try Chinese cabbage (very fast-growing), tatsoi (same family as pak choi), mizuna (prolific), mustard red giant, Chinese broccoli or choy sum. Or buy a mixed pack of Asian leaves. They can be grown all year around and are very nutritious, providing vitamins C, A and K as well as calcium, potassium and iron.

Mixed salads

Salads are the ultimate crop for small spaces: fast growing, productive and bursting with flavour. Go outside and pick some five minutes before lunch – it really can't get much fresher than that!

You don't need much space, or sun, to be self-sufficient with salad veg. The secret to success is to keep sowing them in seed trays so that you always have a supply of baby plants to move into containers when the old plants get tough or bitter. You can grow salads as cut-and-come-again plants (see page 60), or allow them to grow into full-headed lettuces, etc.

Early carrots

Long carrots can be tricky to grow, but 'baby' carrots (and the round varieties) are easy and very quick. Sow them where you want them to grow, and gradually thin them out to the spacing recommended on the packet. They'll be ready to harvest in about eight weeks.

Dwarf French beans
There are two types of bush varieties that are the best, including 'Derby' and 'Provider'. Both of these are perfect for your plot as they only need soil 30cm deep to grow in. For plants like these, this is where the use of canes and potentially the use of an adjoining wall come into play – beans want to reach for the skies, so make sure that you allow them to climb to achieve their full potential.

Radish
Radishes can be grown quickly and easily, even if you have the smallest container. All you have to do is scatter some seeds on the top of the soil in your container and diligently keep the soil moist.

Swiss chard
Also known as rainbow chard, this is a spectacular vegetable that wouldn't look out of place in an ornamental garden.

Swiss chard grows all year round; the small leaves look beautiful in salads and the big ones taste delicious cooked – the stalks, in particular, have a similar taste to asparagus. It can be kept as a perennial, and if you keep picking the outer leaves more will grow so you can keep harvesting one plant for months.

Tomatoes

Few things taste as good as a home-grown tomato – it's a total taste sensation! They are also one of the most productive crops you can grow in containers – 5kg from one plant is common. Each plant crops for a long period, giving you fresh tomatoes over several months. You can grow all sorts of colours and varieties at once, such as 'Tigerella' (full tomatoes with speckled orange stripes), 'Amish Paste' (plum droplet-like tomatoes, much like cherry tomatoes in size) or 'Cherokee Purple' (dark mahogany-red fruit, similar in size to beef tomatoes). There are so many to choose from – from the traditional red to yellow and even black, and in any size – from cherries to plums to beefsteak. Tomatoes look and taste incredible in salads, and also taste great dried or cooked.

Edible flowers

These are all beautiful flowers in their own right, and will attract the pollinators which are so important in your garden, but aside from that they are also all edible and look fantastic added to a salad for a burst of colour and flavour. Try nasturtiums, pansies, *Bellis perennis* (daisy), *Calendula officinalis* (marigold), bergamot, elderflower and borage.

Your planting plan

Here are four planting plans that you could use in your space. We came up with these plans using the main problem areas that people usually have, which are not a lot of time for watering or maintenance and a shaded area in which to grow. I have also included a plan here that features crops which are pretty trouble-free in terms of pests and diseases. We thought these plans would cover most bases for everyone, but of course each space is different so feel free to chop and change the plants as you experiment with your own plot and your own preferred tastes.

→ **Easy and Bountiful** – as the name suggests, this is a plan that is easy and bountiful and is most productive in a site that has plenty of sunlight and water.
→ **Low on Light** – for spaces with limited sunshine.
→ **Fast Food** – good if you want a quick turnaround from sowing to eating.
→ **Perennial Possibilities** – a plot that will keep you going for years and years with minimal work!

Hopefully this covers most requirements, but obviously you don't have to stick to this rigidly. Be inventive and creative and come up with your own planting plan. For example, why not grow your beans up your sweetcorn – one of the first companion planting ideas was the 'three sisters' method which involves growing sweetcorn, squash and beans simultaneously in the one patch of soil. The theory behind this is that the corn acts as a climbing support for the beans, the beans

fix nitrogen into the soil and thus add to the soil fertility, and the squash provides ground cover to help reduce water evaporation and can help stop weeds, too. Alternatively, you could grow something tall with a small root system alongside something smaller but with a larger root system in rows (known as intercropping or bi-cropping) such as Brussels sprouts alongside carrots – their roots shouldn't interfere with each other and they should mask each other's odours to possible aphids and pests that are out to eat them.

Essential kit

Here is a list of what you'll need to bring these plans to life. All of the following can be found around the home or for free in your local area (see Chapter 2 for tips on recycling and upcycling):

→ Sticks/canes/lengths of wood to support your beans or tomatoes as they climb. These work well with all the planters we mentioned in chapter 2 when you are looking to increase the capacity of your growing space. These also add height to allow crops to maximise space by growing vertically.
→ Twine/old wire/old shoelaces to tie your plants to their supports. For instance, when growing plants in the standard planter you may need to tie squash, tomatoes or beans (delete as applicable) into a certain position to reach the light or to control them and prevent them suffocating other crops, and to help them support the weight of all the fruit they have growing on their stalks.
→ 2-litre plastic bottles, cut in half to use as little 'cloches' to help germination of seeds by creating a mini greenhouse (warm atmosphere, moist if kept watered) or to help prevent attacks on your plants by birds, slugs or snails. For example, the tender plants in planting plan 1, such as young courgettes or cucumbers, may need your protection in the early days after planting out because these are Michelin-star food to slugs and snails.

Some crops will not come as seeds, but as something called tubers instead– potatoes come in this form. They are baby versions of the main crop, seedlings if you will. You should take these and let them 'chit', that's right, you read correctly. 'Chitting' is a way to get the tuber ready for planting. You know that time you leave potatoes in a cupboard for a while and they grow shoots? Well those are exploratory stalks looking for the surface of the soil, the potato has chit! (Not sure whether you can turn this into a verb, but there you go!)

Once your potato or Jerusalem artichoke has grown these stalks to around 10cm they are ready for planting. That's all you need to know. These crops are so self-sufficient that they don't require much more of your time. Just plant them and wait for the results.

Spacing

In the planting plans that follow I've indicated the ideal space each crop needs but as I've mentioned already, intercropping means that you can plant lots of crops all together and they will grow wonderfully. Just make sure that each particular tomato or runner bean or whatever is well spaced according to the next crop of the same type. As you can see from the plans, I've worked all the crops into a big, collaborative 'mess' so don't be too precious with spacing: if something isn't growing well you can always move it slightly!

Planting plan no. 1 – Easy and Bountiful

This plan is for those who are keen to get really involved in this growing lark but haven't done it before – and have a lovely sunny spot for their planter. The following crops should be very easy to grow provided they get enough sun, plenty of water and a little bit of your time and TLC.

Plot make-up

→ At least 6 hours of full sun
→ Plenty of water
→ 2–3 hours a week of your time
→ Eating your veg within 30–40 days

Plants you'll be growing:

Vegetables	Seeds	Resow	Space
Peas	6–8	4 wks	7.5cm
Runner beans	4–5	n/a	2/25cm
Courgette or cucumber	1	n/a	n/a
Tomatoes	3–4	4 wks	50cm
Chard (Quick Cropping)	6	8 wks	15–20cm
Beetroot (QC)	6	2 wks	10cm
Chillies	1	n/a	n/a
Squash	1	n/a	n/a
Shallots	10	n/a	15cm
Potatoes	6–8	n/a	30cm
Salads (QC)	20	2 wks	2–3cm

Fruit	Seeds	Resow	Space
Strawberries	3-4	n/a	30–40cm

Edible flowers	Seeds	Resow	Space
Nasturtiums	4	n/a	n/a

Herbs	Seeds	Resow	Space
Chives	1	8 wks	10cm
Rosemary	1	n/a	20cm
Spearmint	1	n/a	20cm
Thyme	1	n/a	15–20cm

How to approach this plan

This planting plan is perfect if you have plenty of sun and water getting to your plot. Courgettes and other squashes are easy to grow as long as they get enough food and water. Potatoes are very easy but be careful

with spacing as they can spread quite a lot and unlike courgettes and squashes that can have their foliage moved around to suit the grower and the light needs of the other plants, potatoes are soil bound and thus need more space. Salad varieties such as 'Arran' or 'Red Duke of York' (what a fantastic name, btw!) are best for container growing and can be used for everything from salads to chips – they will taste better than your average Maris Piper. Look for 'early' varieties, which produce potatoes very quickly. Remember, home growing means you can choose when you harvest your crops, so pulling potatoes when they are young is fine and encouraged!

Tomatoes and courgettes are happy in containers in a sunny spot. Look for bush tomatoes, as they need less attention. Small-fruited cherry and tumbling tomatoes are particularly quick, easy and tasty.

Spinach can be tricky for beginners, but perpetual spinach or chard are good substitutes that are far less fussy.

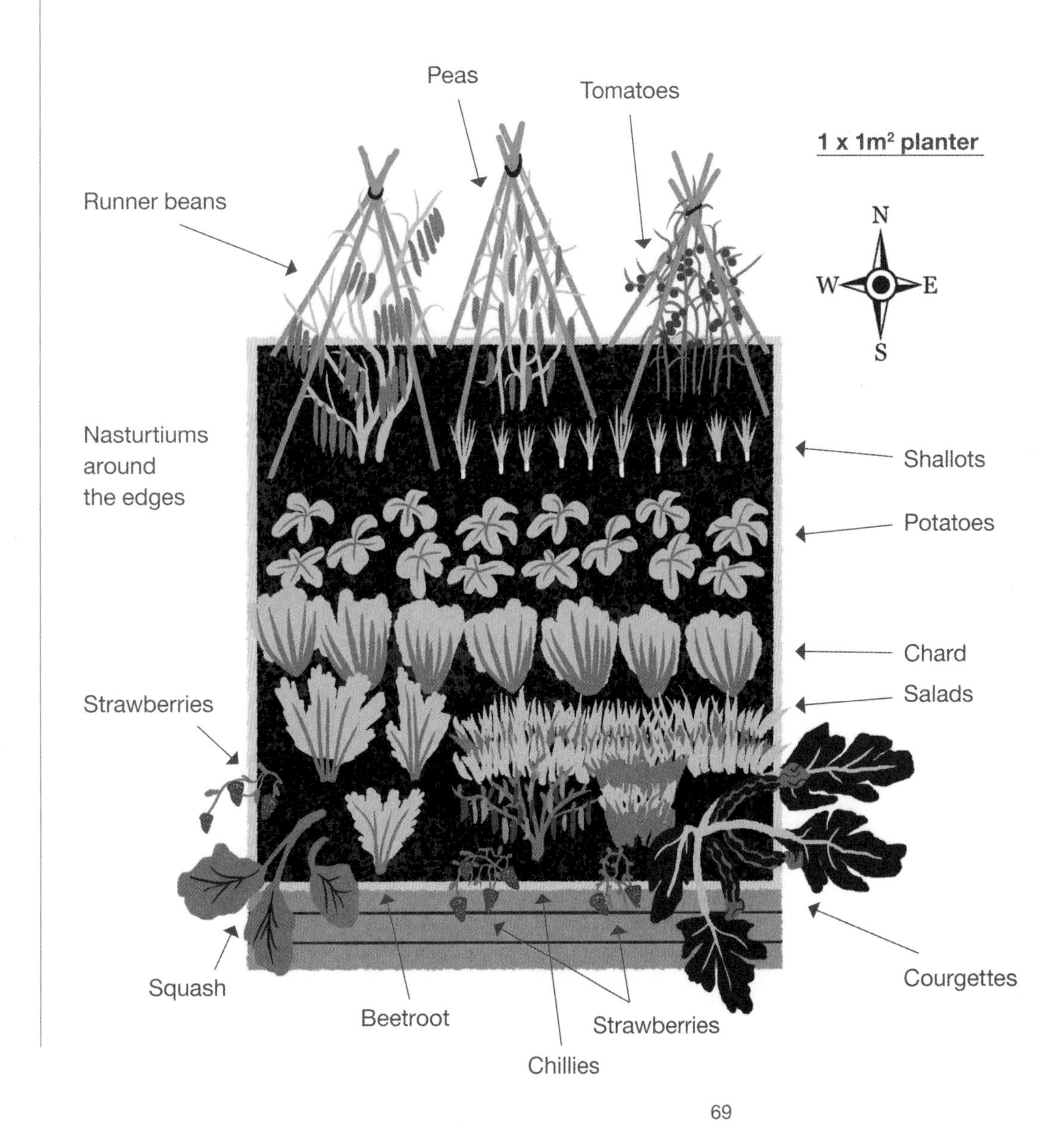

Planting plan no. 2 – Low on Light

This plan is for those who really want to give growing a go but are afraid that the only space they have for a planter is way too shady to grow anything at all. Fear not, we have come up with a plan that should suit you and still grow very delicious and nutritious herbs and vegetables.

Plot make-up

→ At least 3–4 hours of sun (hopefully!)
→ Water every other day
→ 1–2 hours a week of your time
→ Eating your veg within 30–45 days

Plants you'll be growing:

Vegetables	**Seeds**	**Resow**	**Space**
Salads (Quick Cropping)	20–30	2 wks	2–3cm
Potatoes	8–10	n/a	30cm
Broad beans	8–10	n/a	15cm
Beetroot (root and leaf) (QC)	10–12	2 wks	10cm
Radishes (QC)	10–15	2 wks	2–3cm
Kale (QC)	7–10	n/a	30cm
Spinach (QC)	8–10	4 wks	8cm

Herbs (tender and woody)	**Seeds**	**Resow**	**Space**
Sage	1	n/a	25cm
Parsley (QC)	3	8 wks	15cm
Coriander	3	8 wks	15–20cm
Basil	3	8 wks	15cm
Chives (QC)	5	8 wks	10cm

Fruit	**Seeds**	**Resow**	**Space**
Rhubarb	1	8 wks	10cm

How to approach this plan
If your plot is low on sunlight, all is not lost. As we've said before, a lot of crops will do just fine on 3–4 hours of light per day. Generally, the leafy crops such as the oriental greens, spinach, salads and herbs will do the best, so perhaps focus on getting your fruiting crops such as tomatoes and strawberries down at the local farmers' market instead. However, leafy vegetables need a regular supply of water to grow quickly. You could be self-sufficient in salads and greens, though, if you put your mind to it!

Growing salad leaves saves you a fortune on bagged supermarket leaves. Sow a short row (or tray) of seeds every two weeks for a continuous supply. You will find instructions in the following chapter on how to do this (see pages 95–97).

Rhubarb is a great crop that just gets on with growing delicious stems, and needs little to no attention at all, and as a perennial plant it will last and crop from year to year.

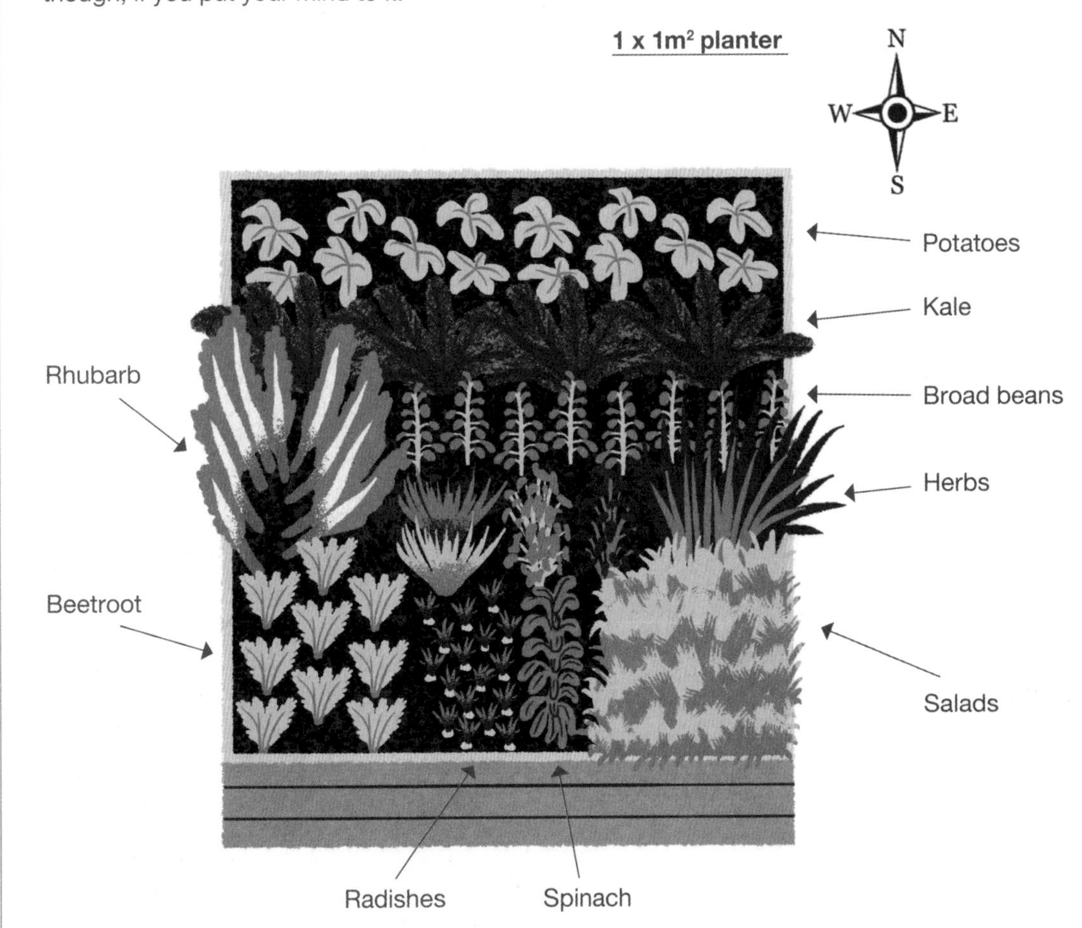

Planting plan no. 3 – Fast Food

If you don't want to be waiting months for a single courgette and would rather see the fruits (literally) of your labour as quickly as possible, this is the planting plan for you.

Plot make-up

- → At least 6 hours of full sun
- → Water every other day
- → 1–2 hours a week of your time
- → Eating your veg within 25–30 days

Plants you'll be growing:

Vegetables	Seeds	Resow	Space
Salads (Quick Cropping)	20	2 wks	2–3cm
Baby carrots (QC)	10–15	2 wks	2–5cm
Pea or broad bean (QC)	8–10	4 wks	7.5cm
Beetroot (root and leaf) (QC)	10–12	2 wks	10cm
Rainbow chard (QC)	8–10	8 wks	15–20cm
Oriental greens (QC)	5–7	2 wks	2–3cm
Nasturtiums (QC)	4–8	n/a	n/a
Cavolo nero (QC)	5–8	n/a	20–25cm
Lettuce, rocket, other salads	20	2 wks	2–3cm
Radishes	10–15	2 wks	2–3cm

Herbs (tender and woody)	Seeds	Resow	Space
Mint	1	n/a	n/a
Parsley	3–5	8 wks	15cm
Coriander (QC)	3–5	8 wks	15–20cm
Chives (QC)	8–10	8 wks	10cm

How to approach this plan
Beetroot is a very easy crop to grow and you can use the young leaves in salads. Beetroot 'seeds' are actually clusters, and each one produces several seedlings. You can snip off the excess seedlings to grow single roots, or leave them to grow into little groups of baby beets. Again, you'll be able to start harvesting after about eight weeks.

Radishes are probably the quickest crop of all – sow the seeds every couple of weeks and watch them spring up. Water them well to avoid woodiness, and harvest them while they're young and sweet.

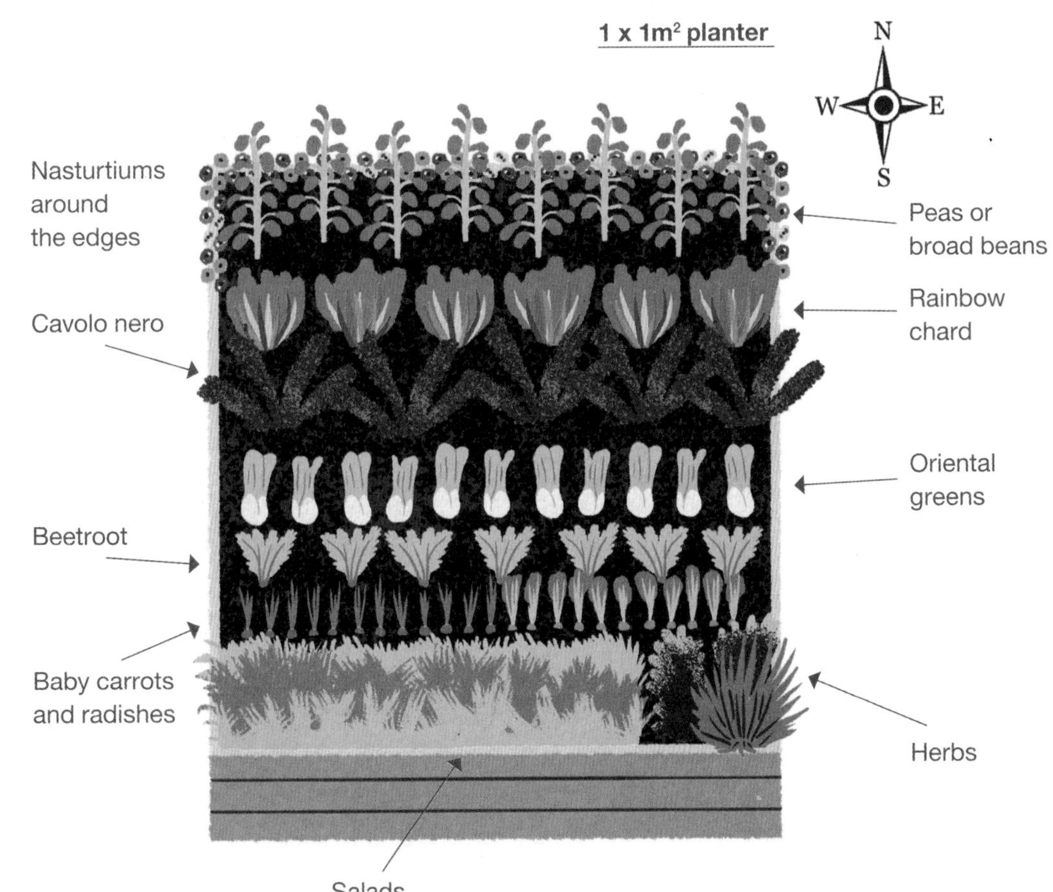

Planting plan no. 4 – Perennial Possibilities

If you don't have a lot of time, or just think that growing annuals is a bit of a waste of energy, then you could grow plants that keep going for years and years, and indeed only get better over time. Some of these vegetables, such as the artichokes and asparagus, will actually need a few years to establish before you can harvest them, but after that they will provide delicious produce for many years. The other vegetables offered here, such as cavolo nero and rainbow chard, should provide you with a crop within a season, but they are perennial so they should see you through many years.

Plot make-up

- → At least 4–6 hours of full sun
- → Water every other day
- → 1–2 hours a week of your time
- → Eating your veg within 25–30 days

Plants you'll be growing:

Vegetables	Seeds	Resow	Space
Asparagus	4–6	n/a	20–30cm
Globe artichokes	1	n/a	n/a
Jerusalem artichokes	4–5	n/a	25–30cm
Rainbow chard (QC)	5	n/a	15–20cm
Cavolo nero (QC)	5	n/a	20–25cm

Herbs (tender and woody)	Seeds	Resow	Space
Your choice	3	n/a	15–20cm

Perennial salad leaves	Seeds	Resow	Space
Chicory or sorrel (QC)	20	n/a	2–3cm

Fruit	Seeds	Resow	Space
Rhubarb	1	n/a	n/a
Strawberries	5	n/a	30–40cm
One dwarf fruit tree	1	n/a	n/a

(alternative to rhubarb, such as pear or apple)

How to approach this plan
Consider using a portion of your plot for perennial crops, such as rhubarb, asparagus, globe artichokes and some herbs. They live for a long time so you'll only need to plant them once to get harvests for many years. They'll also need less watering once they're established, as they will develop more extensive root systems than annual or biennial crops.

Fruit trees, like a delicious apple or pear tree, are a good perennial choice as they keep producing year after year. I'd suggest either going with rhubarb or the dwarf fruit tree. Even if you don't have a lot of space you can grow these – choose a dwarf tree, place it in any container and it will fruit for you. Other fruit, such as strawberries, are perennial too and won't need much attention either.

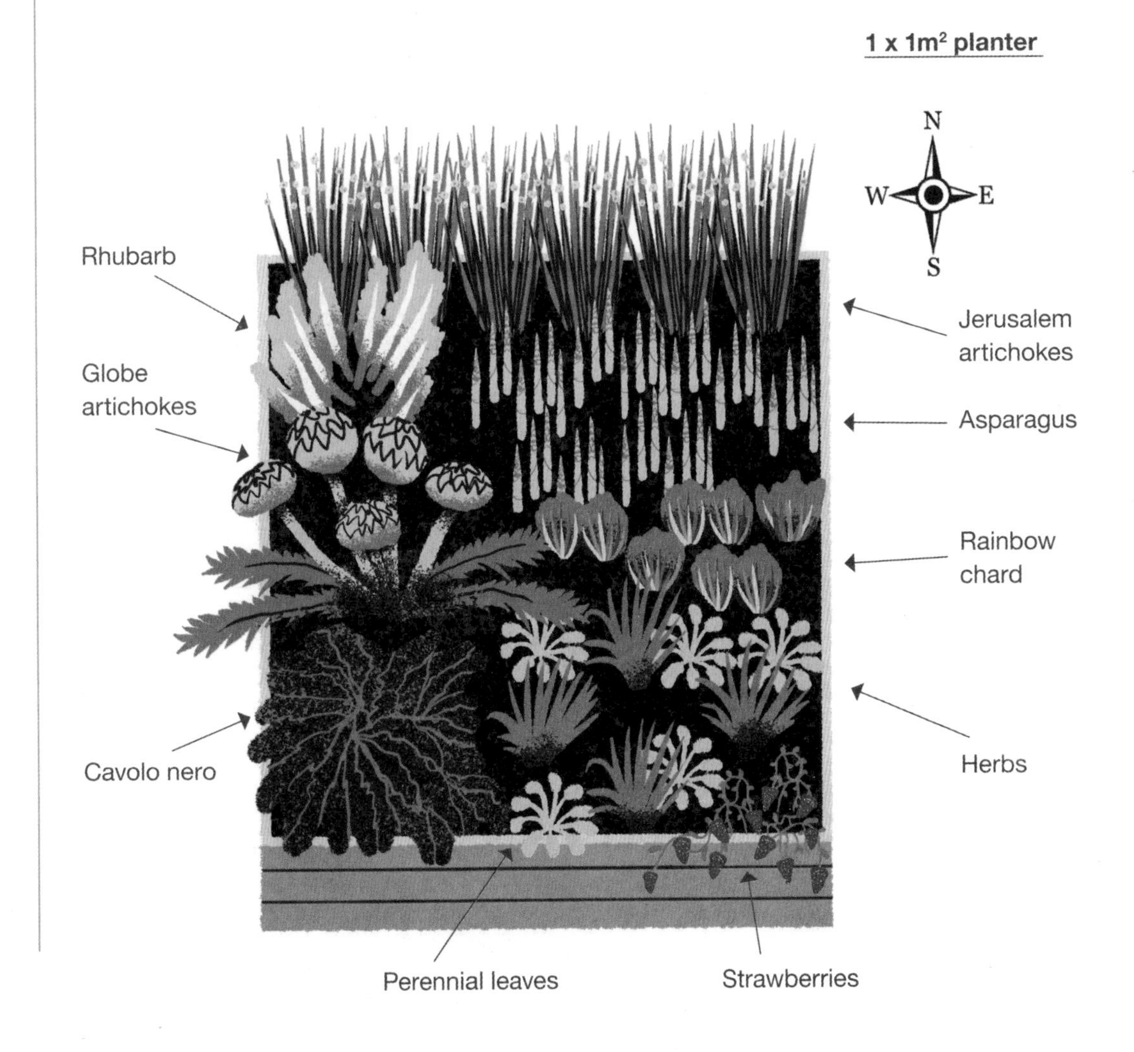

Switching out

If you like what you see in these planting plans but want to introduce something extra to your plot or don't like something we have detailed into the plot of your choice, take a look at these crops which you can interchange with the ones you want to remove. This selection of interesting vegetables and fruits can sometimes be expensive to buy but often taste incredible – all the more reason to grow them yourself.

Runner beans
One of the most productive crops – several kilos of beans can be grown in one pot. The orange or white flowers add beauty to the garden and the height of the plants lends stature. For tender, tasty beans pick them when they are still small, which will also encourage the plant to produce more. Runner beans like a constant water supply and grow best in a container with a water reservoir (see chapter 2 for planter build).

Cavolo nero
One of the most nutritious leafy green crops, cavolo nero is up there as one of the most attractive too. It can be grown as a perennial as it is so hardy that it will survive the coldest of winters in the UK. Sow in spring for a summer harvest or later in the summer for a supply of leaves over the winter. Leaves can be cooked or eaten in salads and are full of flavour and nutrition!

Chillies

As long as you have a sunny spot and love chillies, these plants are a winner. Not only do the plants look great, but home-grown chillies have an added taste dimension of being fresher and sweeter and you can grow them to different sizes and shapes so you can dictate the flavours depending on when you harvest them. One productive plant can give you almost 100 chillies over the growing season, so self-sufficiency in chillies can be a possibility! Any that you can't eat can easily be dried for eating over the winter. Drying chillies is very easy; simply put the harvested chillies on a windowsill in full sun (ideal, but not crucial!) on a piece of kitchen paper and leave them to slowly dry out. Alternatively, using a needle and thread pierce each chilli and then hang the bunch up in a warm room – perhaps your kitchen – and they will dry out over time. You can hasten this process by putting the chillies into a oven that has cooled down a little after cooking – you don't want to cook them, just let the moisture be drawn out. There is no time limit to this, just leave them in the oven as it cools and it should do the trick; take them out when the oven is cold. However, the best way to dehydrate chillies is with the windowsill process.

Peppers

It is an ideal rule to grow peppers in a big pot so that they grow better. This will allow them to grow expansive roots, which are key to growing large, healthy peppers. They do like sun but any sweet or chilli pepper will grow in a container, so could be brought indoors if you aren't seeing much success outdoors or if you need to move it to a greenhouse.

Nasturtiums

The supreme edible flower – bright and radiant in the container garden and it adds a peppery flavour and vibrant colour to salads. The small round leaves and flower buds are also edible. Great for companion planting because they can prevent aphids attacking other crops – in particular anything in the brassica (cabbage) family, and especially broad beans.

Pea or broad bean shoots

The easiest crop to grow and one of the most expensive to buy in the shops! For about the same price as a pint of milk you can grow enough pea and bean shoots to pay for your monthly Netflix subscription in one seed tray in just three weeks. That's about a 900 per cent cost-to-value ratio! If you sow them successively you can have a

never-ending supply. They taste delicious and look beautiful as a garnish or even as the main ingredient of a salad or stir-fry. They can be grown in the tiniest space – even a windowsill would do – and only need about an hour of sunlight each day.

Mixed herbs

Having a never-ending supply of tender or hardy herbs (as detailed earlier in this chapter) can make all the difference to the flavour of your dishes in the kitchen. Mint, parsley, chives, coriander, basil, dill, rosemary, sage and thyme should be on your wish list and can be grown year round, too. They are attractive to pollinators and can be grown as companion plants to help protect other veggies as well. They are complete all-rounders so they won't need too much looking after.

Beetroot

Try to grow 'Red Ace' type. Beetroots like good soil depth for their roots in order to fuel the development of that delicious bulb, so make sure you give them room. We'd only recommend growing these in our standard planter as they will need about a 10cm radius to grow well and then you'll be able to grow up to six different plants. If you want to have more, opt for baby beetroot: just pick them when they are young.

What now?

Firstly, see what you can buy locally. Most of these crops are ideal to grow from seedlings, just requiring you to plug them into the ground, care for them and help them grow. Try to source them as locally as possible because you'll be undoing all the marvellous environmental work you're beginning if you then get in a car and drive miles to buy your plants. It also allows you to support local growers who will be doing wonders in the area for wildlife and the ecosystem with their business.

What you can't source nearby, consider growing from seed yourself or order seedlings online. Growing from seed yourself is much more cost-effective as one seed pack might have as many as 200 seeds in it, which could provide you with many more years' worth of seeds if you're growing in a small plot!

Whichever you choose, order your seeds or seedlings in late winter so that they arrive as early as possible in spring to enable you to grow in as much of the growing season as possible (in the UK this is generally the beginning of March until the end of September, but really depends on the weather and whether or not you are growing indoors as well as outdoors. If you are growing under cover, ie, in a greenhouse, you can extend the growing season at each end of it). Choosing your seeds is something you can do on long dark nights in the cold

winter months as you plan all the incredible meals you are going to eat from your bounty!

Online resources and apps

As we've mentioned before, there are some digital tools (listed on page 138) that you can use to help you get things right, and not forget important key tasks like watering and seedling checking and to plan your plot. Koubachi is a wonder app that is free and you can use it to plot where your plants will go – particularly if you 'calibrate' it (a fancy term for telling the app the preferred growing conditions of your plant, when you sowed it, and so on). Use this to guide your ambition. *permaculture* magazine and intoGardens both have apps that have lots of resources from planning and inspiration to guides that you can use to bolster your crop and learn more about the plants and methods detailed in this book. Garden Plan Pro is a paid-for app that delivers an all-in-one growing toolkit that provides planning and harvesting reminders, which even call on local weather station data to make the information it provides highly personalised. Google Keep is a reminder tool that will help you create a list of all the crops you need to buy seeds for and of jobs you need to do within your plot. It will also inspire you through the photo reminder option; this allows you to add photos to notes, then you can time the reminder and set the date for

4 weeks' time, for instance, and you'll get a photo reminder of just where that crop has come from, to the present date! The best element is that you can set the reminders to be geographically triggered so that you don't need to be conscious of the date but rather when you are in the place you are growing: 'remind me to buy this list of plants when I'm at a certain shop' and bam, up pops the list when you get there!

Websites such as Garden Organic (www.gardenorganic.org.uk) have comprehensive lists of crops and guides that you can use if you need further help to get you through this stage.

Planting:
From nursery
to university

Taking the crops from the day you plant them to the day they graduate to your plate is what this chapter is all about. This is where each planting plan will be explained in detail, including how to support all the crops listed, so that you can give them what they need to prosper.

I will also talk about the process of 'thinning' your seedlings – basically removing the little stragglers so that the largest and healthiest ones have room to grow and achieve their full potential. I will explain why you need to feed your plants and why this is important and discuss the best method for getting your plants to stand on their own...roots, as well as how all the planning and preparation you have done before can come together to support your crops and help you fight disease. To give you a helping hand here, I'll suggest some sacrificial crops you can plant too, so-called because they distract bad insects, and some beneficial crops (see the section on nasturtiums on page 127), which will draw in the best and most helpful insects that nature has to offer.

Whatever you have planted, each crop has an innate desire to reach its own end goal – which is to produce lots of seeds to deliver the next generation of itself. A nice way to think about this is to imagine the crops as cars driving down a road. They each have a final destination that they are aiming for but along the way there will be distractions, dangers and obstacles to avoid and navigate. Each car wants to stay on the road to their destination but some will come up against too many challenges to get there. What I am going to do is blunt and nullify obstacles to ensure that as many of your crops get to your plate as possible.

So far, what you've built and prepared from the previous chapters are the perfect conditions for them to do this.

I think it's worth setting out that this process would happen naturally without human interaction, you are just helping to facilitate a greater return from the crops you sow to produce enough food for us to enjoy regular meals. Each crop will often produce well over 200 times the initial seed that you plant; what you are trying to do is to get a greater harvest from your crops than you would naturally achieve. Easy when you think about it like that, isn't it?

In the planting plans that I detailed in the last chapter, there are companion crops that enhance the planter's sum of its parts, meaning that the plants will work together, often in the same space, to support each other and facilitate more growth. This fantastic method of production will develop healthy crops that deter pests and keep you eating those tasty greens you set out to eat!

Companion planting is a process as old as nature itself; natural habits have evolved to include plants that provide a symbiotic relationship to one another. One plant might improve the soil conditions (such as legumes like peas and beans) for a plant such as

a fruit bush or sweetcorn, which in turn allows climbers like beans to clamber up it. Many plants have a less obvious working relationship but instead discreetly provide others around them with benefits. The allium family (leeks, garlic, onions, etc.) all, as I'm sure you'll know, have a strong taste, but what you may not know is that insects can detect this scent too and several find it very off-putting, including the carrot root fly. This insect, which as the name suggests lays its eggs within the roots of the carrot plant, can decimate an entire crop if left unchecked. Long before pesticides, gardeners discovered that planting garlic and onions around the edge of a patch of carrots led to a much lower infestation of carrot root fly. This easy solution requires no chemicals and

it also provides two lots of vegetables from one plot – a demonstration that companion planting can be very beneficial to small-space growers.

You can use this theory to grow plenty of plants that work together to support each other all over the plot. The plan I have developed uses age-old concepts of plants that enjoy each other's company as well as looking at the plot from an urban grower's perspective: 'how can I make this concept work even better?' The answer here is to evaluate the plot vertically so that plants have the ability to climb, intertwine and hang – so you can see runner beans climbing up sunflowers while both exist in the same soil – allowing them to increase their growing capacity and still work with each other.

What I want to show is that you don't want uniform planting in uniform rows, you want what looks like a mess; something that comes across as a tangle of leaves and hanging plants, something where crops spill over the edges and through cracks in the planter is exactly what you should aim for. It's this natural method that will create the mini urban ecosystem you are after. In there will be food for birds and insects, moisture will be retained by the growing matter and crops will grow on undisturbed.

In this system, if something dies or leaves fall off – let them! They will simply rot down and fuel even more growth. The only exception is when something is diseased – this should be disposed of with your household food-waste collection. You really don't need a picture-perfect image of a garden: it will look like this anyway because of all the great construction work you have done! If something dies, proactively add it to the growing matter. You'll be creating 'lasagne compost' (see page 91), for which all this dead matter can be collected and added to, so that it becomes an ongoing process. Once you have planted your crops, you shouldn't stop adding organic waste to them – keep adding it and your plants will reward you with a bigger harvest.

In the planting method you are employing throughout each of the planting plans, you want to ensure that crops continue to produce food. Naturally, each and every crop that you plant will strive to produce a seed and then die off. You want to limit this or hold the plant in this state for as long as possible. The way to do this is to continually pick the crops as this will fool the plant into thinking it needs to produce more and so it will, continually, until it's exhausted.

This technique is simple and effective and works perfectly in small-space growing. It's an essential part of the growing process. If you overlook this you will gain only small or limited numbers of the produce you want and you'll have to replant the crop again, going through the same development stage from the beginning before you get another crop. From an early gardener perspective, I recommend checking to see if anything is harvestable when you do your daily watering. Don't forget, the advantage of home growing is that you can pick your crops whenever you like. You don't have to wait until they look like they do in the shops, as often the earlier ones are the sweeter and tastier – older crops can get leathery and stringy.

Hay there!

You've built your planter and it looks smashing. You've placed it in the best spot that you've identified from Chapter 1 and you're confident that it will hold together for many fruitful years of domestic horticulture(*). You now need to think about the next stage of the build. This is where you will create the perfect conditions for the crops you are going to grow.

*possibly/possibly not!

The main thing to remember here is that: mess = perfection. Crops will grow best in textured, rich soil that has nutrients and air. Having plenty of air in the soil is essential for good root growth, so you're going to be packing this with lots of different types of organic materials to make it a plant wonderland.

Straw/hay

The first thing that might surprise some of you is that you are not going to be using soil or compost as the majority of the organic material that goes into the planter. Nope, about 75 per cent of what you are going to use will be hay or straw. This will retain air in the planter and provide excellent nutrients as it begins to rot down. These nutrients will be sucked up by the roots of the plants and will fuel lots of lovely plant growth. The straw or hay will also act as a break between the compost and the water reservoir, preventing the soil sagging down into the water.

The difference between hay and straw is thus: hay has the heads of whichever grass has been harvested intact, while straw is what is collected from the field once the corn or wheat (or other crops) have been harvested. Both are good, but because of the seed heads in it hay is that bit better.

The best, and I find most important, aspect of using hay or straw is that it is light, much lighter than soil, and so allows you to move the planter around if you must – particularly if you decided to put the planter on wheels. This is in case you decide to grow on a roof AND because it will save you a small fortune from not having to order a ton of soil.

Make sure you order enough hay or straw as otherwise it will limit the amount of nutrients that the crops will have immediate access to. You don't want to fill the planter fully but have enough to fill it to two-thirds full. The hay or straw should go into the planter first, then the soil/compost will sit on top of this and hold the crops in place. It makes the whole process much quicker, lighter and returns really healthy veg!

How much straw do I need?

→ For the larger planter (see page 46) you'll want two bales of hay/straw – these are approximately 50 x 120 x 40cm each.

→ For the smaller planter (see page 49), you'll likely want just one bale of hay/straw which you'll have to break up to fit it into the planter.

Any surplus straw/hay should preferably be kept somewhere warm and dry, as you'll be able to use this in the maintenance of your plot and to condition the soil for growing season two, next year!

This is one of those areas where I can't provide you with a simple alternative; you really do need straw or hay. If you live near enough to a farm or area of agriculture you could make a trip out, or you can buy it from pet stores or maybe a city farm. However, don't venture too far; this comes back to the perceived wisdom around expending too much effort to obtain the materials; if you drive for 40+ miles to get the hay or straw you should probably reconsider. On this, social media comes to the fore; speak to communities online to see if they know of people or places you can source it from. You can look online to buy it direct, of course. It's fairly easy to find if you search for hay or straw bales but watch out for delivery charges! If you know others who are planning to start growing too, why not club together to gain economies of scale when ordering?

There is no rush for any of this, so ordering online won't jeopardise anything; while the hay is en route you'll be growing and collecting together your seedlings so you'll have something else to focus on.

Growing matter – soil and compost

Good growing matter does not come cheap. The solution is simple: don't use pre-bagged soil for the planter itself, instead make your own.

Think about how nature works: leaves and other plant matter like fruit, a dead branch here or there fall to the ground, then an animal delivers a helping hand as it passes over the same spot, then more leaves fall. This layering process happens naturally – what we're doing is simply creating the same conditions, which in turn creates the ideal conditions for plant germination. The insects churn through it, adding air to the rotting matter and as things begin to break down, nitrogen and carbon are released which all plants lust after to have vigorous growth. It may look awful but the worms love it and so will the seeds and seedlings that you plant.

The most important element of growing is your compost and soil. If you use poor growing matter you will get poor fruit and vegetables. Lesson number one: you want really rich, full-of-organic-life soil to give your crops the best start and take them through to a healthy end. Think of it like baby food;

you want food packed with nutrients and vitamins to deliver a strong foundation for the child. Crop growing is no different.

Creating your own growing matter is fun and easy. It'll take you back to when you were a kid and you just messed about in the dirt, adding things like sand, weeds and water... Just me? Thought not! Again, this will have you drawing on lots of resources that are classed as rubbish and are freely available around every city I've ever been to.

Lasagne compost
You'll need:

→ Old cardboard or newspaper
→ A week's worth of food waste, with no meat or fish
→ Rainwater (can use tap water but rainwater is hugely preferable – see page 26 for more)
→ Leaves (ideally rotted)
→ Teabags/leaves and/or coffee grounds
→ Horse, cow or chicken manure (rotted) – optional (but AMAZING if you have it)

We've all tried to make edible lasagne at some point in our lives, some more successfully than others! Well, this is lasagne gardening-style. The plan here is to create this in your ready-made planter. This is going to be the kind of compost that plants dream of, the kind they all hope to get to taste. It will produce stunning, vigorous, productive crops that above all will be wonderfully healthy. But to forewarn you, as this is rotting material it might smell a little bit. So if you are considering growing indoors or have a planter near the back door, do bear this in mind! If the compost does begin to smell, try squeezing lemon juice over it to neutralise the odour.

The process is very easy: you need to start with the base layer – make this a single layer of cardboard or two layers of newspaper. Next you want to add one layer of brown waste and one layer of green waste.

What is in green/brown waste?

Green waste
→ Vegetable scraps
→ Grass cuttings
→ Garden trimmings, such as shrub clippings or grass cuttings – a local park will likely have a composting area (just do a quick check to ensure nobody gets annoyed by your compost collecting) or you could visit a wood or forest nearby to collect old leaves
→ Tea leaves and coffee grounds

Brown waste
→ Leaves (rotted)
→ Manure
→ Cardboard or newspaper

Now all you need to do is layer them one after the other, alternating until you have a considerable pile – one that exceeds the height of the planter sides. The compost will rot down and reduce in height so don't worry that you have built an unruly, unstable mound – it will all become quite manageable.

Advantages of lasagne compost

→ Well, firstly, you don't have to do any digging, ever! You'll just keep adding new layers as you go.

→ This no-dig approach means that you don't disturb the incredible ecosystem that you have created, which provides much better conditions for your crops to be planted into.

→ The layered cardboard or newspaper will suppress weeds, meaning less weeding for you.

→ The layers will hold water within them – you will still need to water but the growing matter won't dry out half as quickly as regular soil. Bonus!

→ All those wonderful, rich, diverse layers are packed with nutrients that crops crave, so you'll need no fertiliser, meaning organic fruit and veg from the off. Congratulations to you.

Recap...

Right, now you have everything you need to get growing. You've got the container to hold the crops, imaginatively sourced and built at minimal cost. You've got the growing medium sorted, with nutritious straw or hay for the roots of your crops to drill down into, and you've created a wonder substance in which to plant your seedlings that will keep them fed and healthy for the growing season. Essentially, you're ready to grow!

Where from? What time? What now?
Firstly, see what you can buy locally. Most of these crops are ideal to grow from seedlings, just requiring you to plug them into the ground and nurture them as they grow. Try to stay as local as possible because you'll be undoing all the marvellous environmental work you've begun if you then get in a car and drive miles to buy plants. It also allows you to support local growers who will be doing wonders in the area for wildlife and the ecosystem with their business.

What you can't source nearby you should consider growing from seed yourself, or you can order seedlings online. Growing from seed yourself is much more cost-effective as one seed pack might have as many as 200 seeds – which might provide you with many years' worth of seeds if you're growing in a small plot!

Whichever you choose, try to get hold of your seeds in late winter and your seedlings in early spring. If you decide on your full planting plan as early as possible it will enable you to cultivate your crops for as much of the growing season as possible.

Cropping
The small plot you have will be a green, productive haven – but only for so long. Once the initial crops you sow reach the end of their lives there will be nothing to eat. This is why you are going to need to produce more seedlings, continually, throughout the growing season. This is not something to

panic about; there are many crops which will give you lots of produce from just one or two seedlings (courgettes, anyone?!), but there are also crops like salads that will need to be re-sown every few weeks to ensure that you get lots of fresh produce for as long as the weather allows.

I can't advocate this approach enough; if you only sow once you'll only see small returns from your efforts (in all likelihood) and little value in the time you have invested. You'll also feel frustrated by the fact that you are visiting the supermarket for fruit and veg that don't taste half as good as your own home-grown versions. The best advice I can give is to set reminders for yourself – every two weeks for salads, for example. All this is detailed in the planting plans (see pages 68–75). Set these reminders about the time you are active in your plot so you can sow directly into the planter. It's not necessary to start all seedlings indoors – if the weather is warm enough most crops, but in particular salads, kale, chard, beans, can go straight into your plot.

Sow now

Take your seed packets and spread them out in front of you. You can now see the year ahead, in food terms. Each of the planting plans is arranged so that you have plenty of crops that will only need one, possibly two, sowings per growing season. Other crops will keep feeding you if you sow regular patches of seeds. Here I'm going to get you started on the first sowing for ALL your seeds. It's then a simple case of repeating this process at intervals as dictated by how quickly you eat that specific crop and how many you want to grow.

Next you're going to use the toilet roll tubes that I suggested you save at the beginning of the book. If you did this from then you'll have lots of spares now. Why toilet rolls, you might ask? Well, these are quite simply the perfect growing containers. Toilet rolls are made from cardboard which retains moisture and will keep soil and roots securely held together, giving the plants a perfect first home. The best bit is that you don't have to tip out the plants when you come to put the seedlings into the soil; you just plug the toilet roll, plant and soil straight into your planter, saving you time and effort!

Plant twice as many seeds as indicated by the planting plan for each crop. This is to account for seeds that don't germinate for some reason and those that die unexpectedly. This is a regular method of planting seeds; to go beyond what is necessary and then only plant the strongest of crops so that you get the best results come harvest time.

Follow these easy steps to bring your seeds alive:

→ Put all the toilet roll tubes/centres you have collected together and arrange them vertically on a small tray – it can just be a block of wood (see photo).
→ Fill them with peat-free compost (you will only want about a 20-litre bag for all your seedlings, which should cost no more than your monthly Netflix subscription and is available from local DIY stores or garden centres).
→ Follow the planting plan you have chosen. Add one or two seeds to each roll (if you are sowing larger seeds, like beans, only add one seed per roll). The rule for sowing is thus: take the seed and push it into the compost to a depth of double its own size – so a tiny salad seed would simply be patted into the compost at the surface.
→ Write in permanent marker pen on the side of the tube the names of the seeds contained within. Also consider separating the tubes slightly so you can distinguish between the different crops you've sown.
→ Gently water your rolls until you have covered all of your seeds and until you have approximately 1cm of water in the bottom of the tray.
→ Move the tray to somewhere temperate (away from any cold draughts/doors). This might be somewhere like a window ledge or even the top of a kitchen cupboard. You can sow outside if the weather is not less than 15°C during the day. This is particularly relevant for successional sowing in warmer months.

All done. You've started growing. All the seeds will kick into life from their dormant state and begin to grow.

'Roll' call
Make sure you set yourself a reminder on your phone to check on the seedlings in a couple of days, because you don't want them to dry out. Make this reminder a recurring event so that you are gently nudged to come back to them every few days. I'd recommend not setting this reminder for a point in the day when you might easily be distracted, for instance when you are rushing out to work or when you are preparing dinner, and go for some time in the evening, say about 9pm when you are likely to be home. That's just me, though, so set it when it works for you and you know you'll have the time to obey the reminder.

The best thing to learn here is that it's never too late to start the process. If you are busy, if you go away on holiday or if you forget, don't worry. Just go out and sow more crops when you remember. The gap between crops can be picked up by the fruits of the other plants you are growing – as long as you are able to eat something from your plot at any one time, it's fine. The planting plans are designed to allow you to have continually harvestable crops; the short-lived ones are there to dot between the larger annuals and perennials.

I'm not advocating a rigorous cropping cycle where, to the minute, you have a new seed in the ground. Not at all. Sow whenever you can; if you sow too many for your plot, don't worry – either share them with friends or keep them growing to one side so that you can find a place to sow them later or in case something in your plot dies.

Seedlings – from seeds to table

The seeds are planted, now there are a few key jobs you need to get them ready for the garden and ultimately to be cropped for the table. These are the straightforward tasks that are sometimes overlooked and can be where all the hard work falls down so use your phone to set tasks and reminders to make your plot the food-producing wonder you hope it will be!

Watering

Take care to maintain the water levels in the tray; don't overwater as you'll drown the seeds, but not providing enough water could also severely hinder your food-growing endeavours. One way to ensure that you do this is by not hiding the growing trays out of sight. You're busy and therefore you have a lot on your mind so you may overlook this very important task if the seedlings are not immediately visible. It might be an idea to write up the task on the fridge or a chalkboard, as well as set digital reminders, or have another member of the family or household take this on for you.

You needn't worry too much about your plants at this stage; their needs are very simple and you are satisfying all of them without too much effort. The cardboard tubes will maintain the compost moisture and help everything progress as it should.

Feed

The seeds will have everything they need at this point to grow on to a plant-able state. The nutrients present within the compost will be ample and perfectly sufficient until you get the seedlings into the planter. If you wish, you could give the crops a simple feed to ensure that they are in really good health when you move them to the larger pot. The next chapter contains a detailed approach to utilising very common weeds as excellent plant feed which will cost you nothing. Using comfrey, nettle or borage 'tea' will see the plants grow rapidly and set roots down with surprising expediency.

As I've said before, feeding your seedlings isn't particularly necessary but you may want to do it if you know you will be transferring them into poor organic matter or a particularly shady spot and want to give them the greatest chance of survival – in these situations feeding will produce bigger seedlings quicker, thus allowing you to eat sooner!

Checking

At this very early stage of growth, you want to ensure the seeds are coming on well, so when you water, just have a look over the many rolls of seeds and seedlings to ensure all is well. Things you might want to look out for are:

→ Some rolls not producing any shoots at all. This is probably because the seeds are too deep in the compost or simply because the seed is still working its way through the soil. You might want to legislate for failure here by sowing some more seeds in new toilet roll tubes. If you do this, you'll either have lots of seedlings to find planter space for or you'll continue as planned – either way you won't go hungry or be disappointed.

→ Too many seedlings in one tube. It happens. Seeds are small and when you sow them you can accidently drop in too many. It's not a bad thing as you'll be able to resolve this with thinning (see below) and can mean you'll have more food than you expected.

→ Having some seeds growing where you didn't expect them to! Some seeds may have missed the appropriate tube when you sowed them or some might have accidently ended up amongst other crop varieties that you've sown. You'll need to move things around if this is the case and plant up errant seeds properly in their own tubes. This will give them the correct foundations to flourish and save you wasting time growing them on to seedlings to plant out when they might not be strong enough to survive.

Thinning

It's an age-old practice, taking out the smaller, weaker seedlings at the very early stages in order for the bigger seedlings to grow strong. It's natural selection with a human helping hand. You NEED to do this. It might seem cruel or counterproductive but

it's essential to get the best crops. Do this around three weeks after you first sowed the seeds.

The process is a simple one: evaluate each tube and see which is the strongest seedling growing in it. If you only have one seedling, move on to the next. By the strongest I mean the biggest, and the one that looks healthiest, with the best initial leaves and shoots.

Once you have decided you can pull out the weaker ones. Either discard them onto the compost pile or attempt to replant them into new tubes of their own. The stress of removal for such a small plant is often enough to kill them outright so beware of pointlessly replanting soon-to-be-dead plants. However, many can be saved so do attempt this if you have the time...and patience!

When you're finished you'll have a single seedling in each roll, almost ready to go into the planter.

Graduation

What now, you ask? Once you've grown and/or purchased all the crops from your selected planting plan it's now time to evaluate the weather: if it's consistently below 8–10°C outdoors, then hold tight with planting out your seedlings, it's too cold. Keep your seedlings where they are and let them bask in the warmth of your home.

Then wait. You can't plant anything when there is the risk of frost. Take a look online to see what the long-range forecast is in your area and plan to get everything ready once you have a consistent nightly temperature of above 8°C. While you wait for this magical number, you should begin putting the finishing touches to your plot – this includes things like plant labels, creating your 'leaf-support' package and taking photos of your seedlings to show off.

Window watching

You live in a city, in all likelihood, so you will be less exposed to the fluctuations of the extremes that weather has to offer and so the chances are good that you'll be ready to plant out once your seedlings are well established.

Before you do this you need to do something called 'hardening off'. This process gets the crops ready to live outdoors by exposing them to wind and outdoor air. All you need to do here is take the tray to a window in your home, put the tray outside on a ledge or the floor and bring it back in in the evening. Easy. Repeat this for 4–5 days. After this time your crops will be ready to go outside.

Many guides will tell you to watch for certain signs to know when you are good to go with your annual crop planting. There are many techniques and methods you can employ. I'm going to plump for a single date against which I can be confident that you'll have no troubles; the date I want you to work to is the first day of spring, PLUS 10 days! Google it to see when it is in your part of the world. Many gardeners and food growers might suggest a different date but I want to make this process as simple and painless as possible. I don't want you to have to cover your crops from bad weather, protect them from frost or have to resow. I want them all to go in together on a certain date that I'm confident will produce a great bounty of crops for you.

Look over the plot

This is where you begin to combine all the efforts you've put in with your build and the work you did to create the ideal plot. Add plant markers (made from wood offcuts or bamboo) to figure out your planting plan. It's all detailed on the plan, including the ideal space each plant needs, so refer to that as you go along. Here is where we at Connected Roots are on hand again – take a look at our Pinterest account, I've added profiles of the plants on the plan (with links to larger pictures if you need them) to ensure you get the full detail. You may have put your plants in a different order but don't worry, it'll work itself out. It doesn't matter if it looks messy; nature has a way of making it work, you just need to concentrate on supporting good plant growth by feeding regularly and watering consistently.

Transplanting

Here we go! Seedlings-in-the-ground day. First things first, go and wet the compost you've made to make sure that you give the seedlings the best start. When I say wet, I mean drench it. Now take your seedlings and place them on top of the soil where you want them to go. This is so that you can see where you might have gaps in the planter and can also ensure that nothing is too crowded. When you have everything spaced out as you would like and as our planting plan suggests, start digging into the soil to make a hole for all your crops. One of the best ways to do this is to use an old branch or stick; it should be about 3–4cm in diameter. I advise using this because you want to disturb the growing matter as little as possible and I want you to exert as little effort as possible. This technique will make a small opening into which you can pop the seedling, bed it in and move on.

Push the stick into the compost and move it around in a circle, creating a hole large enough for your seedling/toilet roll combo. Add the seedling, bed it down into the soil and repeat. Remember, you don't need to take the seedling out of the toilet roll, just pop the complete (and probably quite soggy) seedling into the hole and firm the compost matter around it so that it holds the plant and encourages the roots to begin exploring their new territory.

Once everything is planted, give it all a good watering – and now you're growing! You're officially an urban farmer, helping yourself, your family and the environment.

At Connected Roots we help with Q&As on all our planting plans throughout the year so check our social media channels for more details (see page 138).

Schedule for sowing and planting over 1 month

Follow our timetable for Plot/Build/Plant stages and you'll have nothing to worry about. You might want to photocopy this page from the book and put it on your fridge/cupboard for reference.

New class

The main rule you need to follow to have lots of crops to harvest right through the growing season is to sow regularly. The reason you need to keep sowing seeds is because several of the plants you will have already planted have quite short lifespans. In order to keep you from going hungry you'll need to keep on producing lots of new seedlings for more crops. This may seem an obvious triviality but it's something that a lot of people miss or forget to do. The regularity of planting lends itself to a fortnightly or monthly routine and life can get in the way.

You should think of your job as only half done when you plant that first crop of seedlings. The next day (or even before you plant the first batch of seedlings) you should sow the quick-cropping varieties again. I have marked the quick-cropping varieties on the planting plans so you can easily distinguish them. It should take only 5 minutes to do; an easy task that has its own reward in just a few weeks.

With this approach, when you see that the plants you originally planted are going to seed or turning yellow and dying back, you'll have your secondary set of seedlings ready to go into the planter. The efficiency and effectiveness of that small task will seem huge in comparison to the time it took to sow the seeds in the first place.

And repeat

Do it again and again. Keep doing it through to the end of the growing season. This is the point where you begin to ignore the seasons...to an extent. You are likely to live in a city, which means it will be warmer than the surrounding countryside and therefore you can cheat the encroaching winter weather for a few extra weeks. Make use of this by keeping the food coming right up until the weather tells you that you can't grow any more. You can grow with salads through to the first frost (at this point you can cover your crops to extend their lives further still!). And if you live somewhere that rarely sees a frost then you can experience year-round growing.

This plan combines key tasks from the plot, build and planting chapters all in one so you can see how it all comes together.

Day	Plot task	Build task	Grow task	Time spent
1 - Monday	Plot review: measure spaces around home and visit CR social		Think about what you want to eat!	10 minutes
2 - Tuesday	Plot review: evaluate light conditions – wheels on planter?		Think about what you want to eat!	10 minutes
3 - Wednesday	Plot review: check access to plot – wheels on planter?		Order or buy seeds/seedlings	10 minutes
4 - Thursday	Plot review: think about where you'll get water from			10 minutes
5 - Friday	Plot review: think about safety and security			
6 - Saturday		Pick up cones/ wood to help grow vertically	Sow seed in toilet rolls	15 minutes
7 - Sunday		Think about rainwater collection (see pages 25 & 32)	Sow seed in toilet rolls	15 minutes
8 - Monday		Look for pallet on way home	Water seeds/ seedlings	5 minutes
9 - Tuesday		Look for pallet on way home	Water seeds/ seedlings	5 minutes
10 - Wednesday		Pick up nails/ screws on way home from work	Water seeds/ seedlings	20 minutes
11 - Thursday		Look for wood in skips, etc.	Water seeds/ seedlings	10 minutes
12 - Friday		Speak to scaffolders on way to/from work	Water seeds/ seedlings	10 minutes
13 - Saturday		Visit/call scaffold yard in morning	Water seeds/ seedlings	1 hour

14 - Sunday		Buy polythene and membrane	Water seeds/ seedlings	20 minutes
15 - Monday		Ask friends to borrow tools for this weekend	Water seeds/ seedlings	5 minutes
16 - Tuesday		Buy tools if you want/need	Water seeds/ seedlings	10 minutes
17 - Wednesday			Water seeds/ seedlings	5 minutes
18 - Thursday			Water seeds/ seedlings	5 minutes
19 - Friday			Water seeds/ seedlings	5 minutes
20 - Saturday		Build planter – see chapter 2	Sow more seeds and water other seedlings	30 minutes – 1 hour
21 - Sunday			First day of spring	5 minutes
22 - Monday			Check to see if your seedlings need thinning (see page 99)	
23 - Tuesday	Quickly recheck plot – is it still the best spot to grow? Check drainage – move planter if not in right spot		Collect materials for lasagne compost	
24 - Wednesday			Collect materials for lasagne compost	
25 - Thursday			Save/collect old newspapers	
26 - Friday			Find and collect hay/straw and manure if possible	
27 - Saturday			Make lasagne compost in planter if possible	
28 - Sunday			Keep watering	
29 - Monday			Keep watering	
30 - Tuesday			P Day – get those plants in the ground!	

Winter is coming

And so it ends. The joys of spring and summer are replaced by short days and low temperatures. This is nature's way of saying 'go indoors', but before you do, sow your winter vegetables. I would suggest using the date of the autumn equinox to measure when to sow your winter vegetables (again, Google it for this year's date). The trick is to get the seedlings into the ground before the winter frosts hit so that the plants are established and can tolerate the extreme weather. With this in mind, take your winter veg seeds and sow them separately to your regular seed-sowing activities. Leave them to grow to a healthy size indoors; remember that these are not quick-cropping and will need more time to get to a size where you can take them outside and expect them to survive the rigours of winter weather.

I want you to think about the time you'll dedicate to winter crops, they don't need much, certainly not as much as summer crops, but will still require you to continue maintaining and harvesting in the depth of winter. Seriously think about whether you want to try this… Still keen? Right then, here are some simple crops you can grow:

Broad bean
This is sown straight into warm autumn soil where it will slowly germinate, sit out most of the winter and then pop up to give you an early crop in late winter or early spring.

Chard
Colourful and very hardy, chard will fight on through the winter and keep providing you with a leafy supply through to spring. Sow indoors and plant out in late autumn so it can get established and then simply pick leaves and keep feeding it to get more back!

Spinach
Look back to the planting plans with spinach. Treat it like a salad crop and keep picking it frequently to keep leaves coming. Be wary of taking too many leaves and killing the plant. The cold weather helps keep the plant from going to seed so it's a good one to grow through the winter.

Kale/Cavolo Nero

Again, refer to the plans here. Kale is sturdy and will keep on giving you successive croppings through the darkest of winter months before going to seed as soon as the weather warms. Look for colours and varieties that suit your preference and your palette. Sow indoors and plant in autumn so that there is a healthy, strong crop by the time the poor weather hits.

You can see that I've a preference for leafy crops with decent flavours here. Your plot won't be abundant in winter so the crops you harvest should be distinct and give bold textures when eaten.

Size matters

Your winter veg are going to need to be big enough, and therefore strong enough, to endure the inclement outdoor conditions. The size of seedling I'd suggest aiming for is about 10–15cm in height. If the winter hasn't arrived yet and you are still enjoying your summer bounty, transfer the winter veg seedlings to larger pots so they can continue to expand their roots. Do this by simply plugging your seedling/toilet roll combo into a larger pot of soil. This might now be too big for your home so keep outside under some clear polythene until it's ready to transfer to your planter. This will ensure that you produce really healthy crops that are surging with life when they meet their final growing spot.

The job you have here is one of delicate and considered cultivation, bringing these crops up until you open the door and release them into the wilds of the urban environment. You need to give them more love and support than you would the other summer crops as the conditions they will be going into will be harsh, so it's important to give them the very best start. Focus on their size as the indicator to when they are ready to plant out; missing the autumn equinox is okay as there is always one day in amongst the winter misery when the conditions are acceptable to plant!

Food out of the darkness

Graduation with winter vegetables is a slow process – it may look like you're not getting anywhere and that they are failing, but give them time. These crops are adapted to the lower light levels and colder conditions and will slowly build their root base before offering up a wonderful crop in late winter/ early spring. So don't be disheartened, just wait for all your work to come good and think about how impressed the neighbours will be when you are cropping home-grown produce early in the new year ...

Harvest:
Show me
the marrow

The way I've asked you to plant, all the plants are working together in a tiny ecosystem, supporting each other. This is the companion planting approach I mentioned earlier. It's this simple and progressive approach that means you don't have to do too much work; there's no digging and very little maintenance. I'm now going to give you the tools you need to help your plants grow and flourish.

Your toolbox will consist of:
→ Nutritious plant food
→ Pest traps (not to be confused with animal traps...)
→ Life-sustaining, gravity-fed mini water butts (drip bottles)
→ Kitchen waste

That's pretty much it. It's a fairly basic ensemble really. Everything you need you have around your home or in a nearby green space. I can promise that you won't need to buy anything to gain great crops. Nothing. Good, huh?

The importance of food

It's vitally important to keep feeding the crops you grow because they won't produce half the food that you want them to without it. Think about how you feed any living thing to make it bigger: the better the food, the bigger it will become. You're asking a lot of your crops: you want them to produce lots of food, continually and in a healthy state (I want big tomatoes not tiny green ones). To do this the plant will crave food like a bodybuilder, and it must have the source of it replenished constantly, too. The fuel with which you initiated the growing process (the lasagne compost or other growing matter) will only have enough nutrients for so much growing. This is where you come in: you'll be making a 'tea' from natural weeds – see page 114. Take your comfrey tea solution and be liberal with your use of it. Don't skimp. Don't hold back. Pour forth that watery, smelly mess and let your plants rejoice in the natural, rotten wonder. Remember to do this regularly – 2–3 times a week is fine.

It's okay if you forget once or twice – or even more – because you've built yourself a planter that holds water like no other, that gives back to the plants when they need it, so the water you pour onto the planter will sometimes run all the way through to the reservoir below. This will be returned to the plants when they need it BUT make sure you do try to keep on top of the watering and feeding because you'll be miserable if you

don't, as the plants will draw all the nutrients out of the soil and then not produce anything like the sort of crops they might have if you had kept the feed coming. Keep them growing big and strong and the crop they deliver come harvest time will be immense.

And there is even more added benefit to the planters you designed and built – they will help save the planet! Water wastage is a serious issue, and agriculture accounts for about 70 per cent of the world's freshwater usage, according to the World Wildlife Fund. This is an astounding amount and something that you've now helped to reduce by building your planter so that it wastes as little water as possible. The reservoir holds any surplus water then returns it to the plants when they need it. This process not only saves you time and money but it's great for the environment and your plants benefit from the slow absorption of water – they take their time and get all the nutrients they need rather than being flooded.

Comfrey

I'm not getting all old herbalist on you. I promise! Comfrey is a super weed. It grows everywhere – and I mean EVERYWHERE.

Comfrey is one of those plants that you never notice or think of but once you know about it you won't believe you've neglected it for so long. You often see it growing on wasteland and in forgotten corners of urban areas. Anywhere with just the smallest bit of green space is likely to have some. It self-seeds incredibly well and spreads very quickly unless it is controlled. These are some of the brilliant traits of comfrey, as it is very quickly replenished and comes on with a burst once the cold winter weather fades away.

The final killer trait of comfrey is that it is known as a 'dynamic accumulator', which simply means that it has an excellent capacity for drawing minerals out of the soil and into the roots and leaves of the plant. Gardeners have used this for centuries as a 'tea' to feed their crops in order to deliver the rich mineral that the comfrey plant contains to their crops. It's very good at making crops grow bigger and produce more food; it's like giving crops steroids! Only comfrey is nature's version, it's free and totally natural...and here's how you can use it to do the same.

Go out with a small bag and find the plant in your garden or your local green space and pinch off about two/three handfuls of the leaves. You can identify comfrey from our pictures here or search online for more images as you go on your hunt for this wonder plant.

It couldn't be simpler to turn your bag of leaves into a feed that your crops will love. I have created a quick video guide to this on the Connected Roots Facebook page, in case you are in any doubt.

Step 1
If you've got leaves with lots of stem still attached, pinch them off and discard the stem.

Step 2
This is where your bucket of rainwater I asked you to collect on the page 11 comes in.... Well done you if you left it out to catch the rainwater, but if you didn't, fill a bucket with water (preferably rainwater) and put the comfrey leaves into it, pushing them under the surface with a stick. You can anchor them to the bottom of the bucket with a stone or small brick to keep them fully immersed in the water.

Step 3
Try to give the mix a stir every other day to break up the leaves. When the tea is brown and all the leaves have broken down, your feed is ready. This usually takes two weeks. Once it's ready, you'll have high-grade, concentrated plant feed that's all natural, all organic and packed with everything your crops need.

The best way to use this 'comfrey tea' is to add a teacupful to an almost-full watering can every time you water your crops.

Using comfrey doesn't require any particular thought or consideration; you can't overuse it and your plants will simply go about their

growing business if you stop using it. The minerals in the comfrey tea will seep into the soil and be drawn in by the roots of your plants, so make sure you only water the soil – pouring this concoction onto the leaves will do nothing for your cucumbers and kale. Keep your supply topped up by continually adding new comfrey leaves to the mix – about four or five at a time – mashing them down with a stick and working them into the existing mix of rotting organic matter. You will want to keep the water topped up, too (try to keep the bucket three-quarters full), so that you produce a nice tea and not a thick syrup-like material.

Comfrey tea shouldn't be something you really have to think about and you should never pay for it. There are few things in nature that are so heavily abundant but hugely under-utilised and comfrey is one of them.

If you do really have to buy a comfrey tea mix you can get it online fairly cheaply but I'd encourage you to buy comfrey seeds and simply plant them in a small pot by themselves, instead. This will then become your continual supply of wonderfully nutritious feed, and you will never have to go foraging in public parks again! If you can't find comfrey, there are lots of other wild

plant teas that you can feed to your crops to boost their performance. Feel free to experiment with other plants such as borage and nettles, which grow, like comfrey, just as wild and vigorously and have many different varieties all over the world.

** A point to note here is that the process you are undertaking is to encourage the rotting of organic matter. This will inevitably give off a smell as it does so! With this in mind you won't really want to put this bucket right near your back door/kitchen/balcony, so the best thing I can suggest is to move this to somewhere that you visit fairly infrequently, only going near it when you want to use your plant feed. Keeping a lid on it will restrict the smell. You have been warned!*

Holidays can be a bitch when growing your own food

I get it. You want to go on holiday. Of course you do. But your plants really don't want you to. Not one bit.

Now, my parents tend to ask several neighbours to pop by and water their plants if they go on holiday. They live in the suburbs with friendly neighbours and close family. This request is no big deal for them, but in large urban cosmopolitan areas (like the one you probably live in) the transient nature of a large populace comes to the fore; you are unlikely to know your neighbours well, if at all, and your friends might live an inconvenient distance away. BUT fret not my favourite first-time gardeners, I have a couple of tricks to nail this situation.

Trick 1: An old towel

What?! I can hear you collectively cry. That's right, a towel, nothing fancy, and something very uncomplicated. You can use any old bits of clothing here really, as long as they are derived from cotton and are long enough to reach from the bottom of the planter to the top. Depending on the height between the water butt and your plant you may need to experiment with what material you use for this trick. If towelling won't work, try elevating your water container and using paper towelling. You can also use capillary matting, which is affordable and available in most DIY stores, garden centres or online.

This is a wonderful old-as-the-hills trick that uses capillary action to draw water to your food plot. What is capillary action? Well, water is actually adhesive (who knew?!) and will clump together – think about when you spill water onto a worktop and then clean it up with kitchen paper – if you dip natural materials into it water will stick to it because it is adhesive so each molecule will be drawn along the material following that first one. This process keeps happening until the pull of gravity becomes too much. Does that make sense?

You don't necessarily need to understand the science behind it (if you don't, search 'watering with paper towels' or see the Connected Roots Facebook page and blow your mind). This marvel of chemistry will allow you to go away in the knowledge that your crops will be watered...until the water in the reservoir runs out, that is.

Estimated time needed to produce
Less than 1 minute

Step 1
Take a bucket of water and place it near to your growing plot. (Note: This might not work if you are growing on a windowsill and don't have the space. If this is the case, see the next 'trick'.) You want to place some kind of non-transparent lid on the bucket to prevent the water from evaporating and to keep it cool. This bucket should contain rainwater where possible to maintain the organic, full-of-nutrients mantra I constantly bang on about.

Step 2
Take an old towel (or whatever other items made of natural materials you have available) and put one end of it in the bottom of the bucket, then drape the other end up and over the side of the planter, making sure it is in contact with the growing matter (whether that be soil, compost, or the lasagne compost you made earlier in the book).

Done. This should now begin to draw up the water from the bucket and transfer it to the soil. After a few days you'll be able to touch the towel on its run from the bucket to the organic matter and it should be damp. If it's not, check to see if your towel is still touching the water in the bucket. If this doesn't resolve the problem, skip to trick 2. The best approach is to employ this technique about 1–2 weeks BEFORE you go away on holiday to test that it works.

Trick 2: Drip water bottles

Long weekends are the preserve of the urban dweller; getting out of the city or going on short trips is what us modern folk do, but even a short holiday like this in the heat of summer can be a death sentence for your lettuce or tomatoes. What you need is a quick-to-implement trick that will last the weekend and keep water slowly being fed to your plants while you're on that break to Berlin/Auckland/Darwin (delete as applicable!).

Estimated time needed to produce

Less than 2 minutes

Step 1

What you need to get hold of is a plastic bottle with a lid. It doesn't matter what size or shape, but if you are going away for 2–3 days, a bottle of at least 500ml will work perfectly. You might want to upgrade to

a standard 2-litre bottle depending on where you are and what weather is expected while you're away. The large drinks manufacturers will all satisfy this need. Take it, wash it out and fill it with some of your collected rainwater and comfrey tea at a ratio of 9 parts rainwater to 1 part comfrey tea. Take the lid and make a few small holes in the top – just a few millimetres wide. Screw the lid on the bottle and you're ready to go.

Step 2
Now, just push the bottle into the soil lid first. Bury the bottle up to a third of its height in the soil. This will keep it stable and stop it from falling over but will also allow gravity to do its work.

Step 3
Now saturate the soil around the bottle, making sure you check below the surface of the soil to ensure that the water is getting down to the roots, so that you know it is indeed getting a good soaking.

And you're done. The water will drip out of the bottle over the next few days as the soil near the lid dries out. Now go find your passport and have a good time!

Tricks one and two could be used in conjunction with each other, especially when the weather is hot and no rain is forecast. You should trial these methods before you go away to oversee the experiment and see how effectively they work in your plot, rather than leaving it set up as you go away and hoping for the best, otherwise it could all end badly.

You might need to use several drip bottles strategically placed around your food plot to water with this method. It's all a matter of trial and error. Depending on the size of the bottle and the size of your plot, you'll probably get coverage of 30–45cm^2 from one bottle, so double or triple up where necessary.

Three steps for maintenance

Kids/that last-minute urgent work thing/ your cousin's wedding – things get in the way of having lots of time to look after your plants. Normal gardening books will offer lots and lots of information on the nuances of garden maintenance. You don't need all of this, partly because you want to enjoy the experience and secondly because you don't have the time to dedicate to it.

Instead, I am going focus on the essentials of getting a crop to harvest. You aren't intending to win any prizes with your green beans, you just want to eat them. This section will show you how to work your fruit and vegetable plot to the maximum and still keep everything organic and tasty. I'll guide you as to how to do this simply and quickly to make your food-growing ambitions work around your busy life, rather than the other way around.

My intention is to take away the sudden spikes of necessary attention that your plot demands and rather make it a consistent and steady line of growth that results in convenient crops on schedule. Granted, there will be the odd occasion when something needs looking into, but this hopefully will take just a couple of minutes and you'll be able to do it at the end of the day. Stress free and high reward growing.

The story so far

You've planted everything according to the book so you have a rich growing medium, ample water and enough sunlight and feed to set you off in the right direction; all your crops are planted either as seedlings or seeds and you roughly know when the plants are going to need attention. This is now make or break: keep doing the watering and the care and they will grow to be healthy plants that produce lots of food for you; neglect them, and all the effort you've put in so far will go to waste.

First thing to do

Before you do anything else, get a reminder system in place. Use your digital calendar to set up recurring reminders that continue to prompt (for those of us that don't act on the first reminder – I count myself very much in this camp...). The multiple reminder is handy in case you are busy and then forget. Set this right through to late autumn and add friends to reminders during times when you are away so that they can pop by in case of extreme weather. Make sure to ask them first!

Now go online and find the wonderful tool IFTTT.com. This is going to be a revelation if you've never used it before (I have a video of our set-up on the Connected Roots YouTube page, or our Facebook and Twitter have the video, too, if you want to go there instead!).

This digital tool will connect two very disparate things together for your benefit. When on the site, use the search bar to search the term 'garden' and discover a host of results for the horticulturally minded. The ones you need are those concerned with temperature, rainfall and freezing weather (this latter one you are unlikely to use straight away but it can just sit quietly in the background until it becomes relevant).

Dependent on the climate you're faced with and the water collection system you have in place, you'll likely know quite precisely when you need to come to your crops' rescue because of this tool.

This tool takes much of your weather watching out of your hands as you'll be informed 24 hours in advance of any significant changes in conditions, meaning you can react when your schedule allows and take necessary action. This also means that you are likely to need to do much less watering; you'll be fully aware of how much rain there has been lately (just by checking your email inbox – I find that when it last

rained is something I often completely forget about, like when I last took a taxi or the name of the author of the book I'm currently reading...!).

Follow the steps and set yourself up on the site. Take care to ensure you aren't bombarded by emails by having too many alerts set up because this is where email blindness can be your downfall. If you want, you can connect these alerts and reports to fill out a digital spreadsheet that you can tabulate to see exactly when rain has fallen to improve your watering efficiency – but this is a level of geekery that isn't essential!

Second thing to do

Your battle with aphids, slugs and snails (as well as other pests that might be present in your country or climate) will be never-ending. They are truly industrious and tenacious little blighters. We've all buckled in the past and used pellets – I'm ashamed to say I have – but the ambition to succeed and the desperation to prevent them destroying months of waiting, watching and hoping can drive anyone to overreact. What I'll give you is a kit to help nature fight nature for you. I promise you it feels fantastic to be playing a positive role in nature rather than adding chemicals to the ecosystem you've created. Remember, nature got by without us and it works perfectly without us. Trying to command nature to do something will never work and will usually fail before long. Nature

has a raft of easy solutions for food growers and there are natural predators that will do your work for you, if you let them.

Coffee grounds (and tea)

The most popular drink on the planet is also a rich organic compound that is a good fertiliser – plus slugs and snails dislike it A LOT. They will refrain from crossing it, preferring to go around it. Herein lies a super-quick and easy to obtain pest deterrent.

What you need to do is save the used coffee grounds and old teabags from your regular routine. Set up a jar in the kitchen or at work and tip them in every time you make a brew. (This only works if you make coffee with real coffee, though, not granulated.) Just throw it all in and once a week delve in with rubber gloves and rip open the teabags, empty out the contents into the jar and put the empty bags in with your food waste rubbish. The teabag is biodegradable but it will look unsightly on your veg patch, plus the tea leaves won't be able to rot down as quickly as you want if they are still compacted in a bag. Scatter this mixture around the base of your plants to act as a deterrent to slithering pests.

Copper

Copper is great in your wires and slugs and snails would prefer it to stay there as they really don't like it. You can buy a small roll of copper wire or tape from most

stores on the high street. Now I know I said you didn't need to buy anything for maintenance, and you don't; this trick is an added extra if you are really struggling with pests eating your crops and need to call in reinforcements. You'll hopefully find that the other bits you offer as deterrents do the job, but the most important thing is not to use chemicals, so if you are going to spend money, use this instead!

Create a barrier all around the top of your planter, fix it a little lower than the top edge by unrolling the wire/tape and nailing it to the planks. The pests won't cross it, but make sure no foliage hangs down and gives them a bridge to get across to your succulent greens. If your planter is in a publicly accessible space I'd recommend putting the copper strip just inside the edge of the planter but away from the soil, so it is out of sight of passers-by, as copper has quite a resale value...

Slug traps

When you are doing your bit for the environment and putting out your recycling, be sure to save small shallow containers, as you'll be able to use these to trap slugs and snails in. You can also simply cut out the bottom of small drinks bottles and use these just as easily. You need a knife for this so be careful when cutting through the plastic. Just like the rest of us, slugs enjoy the odd tipple now and again. Well, in all honesty, slugs and snails are mad for the stuff. Put a drop of alcohol such as beer or cider (you don't have to use good booze, anything will do – any liquids that ferment, like orange juice, will work) into the container and lower it into the soil so that the top of the container is just level with the top of the soil. The pests will forget your greens and make straight for the good stuff, tumble in and won't be able to get out. The more pests that head in, the more the scent will get out and the more pests you'll trap. All you then need do is to intermittently empty out the contents for

the birds to come and eat. In effect you're providing yourself and the local wildlife with more to eat. Win-win!

Nasturtiums

There are some things that nature offers which deliver such a potent impact with a variety of uses that you'll wonder how people don't all know about them. Nasturtiums are like this. This wonderfully tasty, quick-growing, ground-covering, climbing hanging plant is very easy to grow, and once you grow it one year it will self-seed so you'll probably never have to replant it.

These flowers are included in the majority of planting plans for good reason, because the leaves and flowers have a great peppery flavour when added to salads and will grow vigorously in almost any conditions. The best way to grow them is to have them tumbling out of the planter, giving vibrant colour to the plot. They also add something for wildlife to savour, as they are a great source of food for bees.

Nasturtiums also have another key trait: they are a draw for a multitude of pests, particularly aphids – greenfly and blackfly. These horrors will prey on your delicate crops without mercy and often end the lives of struggling seedlings. This causes much annoyance and sets you back as you'll need to replant. Nasturtiums are like chocolate to kids at Easter – aphids will go crazy for them. They are drawn to them, which means that if you sacrifice your nasturtiums to them they will leave your other crops alone in order to get their fix.

Now you might think, well, if I don't plant nasturtiums in the first place, the aphids won't come. That might be the case, but when you factor in city growing, where green space is limited and there is much less food for pests, they are likely to arrive anyway so your best bet is to have a first line of defence against an infestation. Planning to encounter them is always the best approach because then, even if they don't arrive, you'll have a great crop of tasty nasturtiums to add to your meals.

Harvesting

The huge benefit of growing your own crops is having the choice of when to harvest your food. Shops have forced us to conform to certain fruit and vegetable sizes, shapes and tastes. When you grow your own food you can break this rule all the time. Some of the best things you will eat will be crops that are picked early or left a little later. Crops like courgettes and cucumbers have an incredible sweetness when picked early that is often lost when they reach 'standard' size. This process also enables you to bring fresher, tastier flavours to your family so that they find out how great veg can taste when they're home grown.

Another benefit is the ability to work different vegetables into meals in different ways, such as using baby courgettes whole in stir-fries or being able to add very young crops like red cabbage or beetroot to salads as a topping to give a tasty punch to the dish. Your options are infinite and the flavours are there to be discovered. With home growing you can explore and not worry that you've wasted a crop if it doesn't taste right; more will soon be available so just keep on trying and tasting!

There is no written rule for when to pick crops, and as to my opening point on this subject, just do it when it looks edible. That said, it is worth taking into account a few things: if you're growing a crop with only one or two fruits, like a pumpkin or a young globe artichoke, these crops are often sold in the sizes and shapes you see them for a reason: it's because that is when they have the most food to offer. You can, of course, pick them sooner but the results may be disappointing, so with simplicity in mind stick to convention here unless you want to experiment.

With some crops, like potatoes and carrots, it can be difficult to know whether you can/should harvest because, being root vegetables with their crop hidden under the earth, you might not be able to see whether you have any food there to eat! The best rule here is to look at the part of the plant that is

above ground: are the leaves looking tired and yellow? Has the plant started to droop? Do the leaves look huge and overgrown? You may only have one of these signs or several. If you have two or more of these signs then chances are that abundance lies just below the surface. It's a simple rule to apply but it's something you can use as a guide to the plant's harvest-ready status. You will know more based on when you planted the crop and when the packet you took the seed from said the plant would be ready.

The best advice for root crops is to harvest them before the first heavy frost comes to kill the parts of the plant that are above ground. Roots are very happy to sit in the ground until you are ready to harvest them but just don't leave it too long otherwise they will rot. The best advice is to dig them up, leave the dirt on them and bury them in a bucket of sand somewhere dry. This will keep them dry and safe until you're ready to eat them. As you'll probably be growing in a small plot you will have a fairly small crop, so just pull the root vegetables as and when you want to eat them. This means that you'll hopefully never leave veg forgotten in the fridge to rot.

By our simplifying standards all this can be condensed into the following evaluation: if you're in the northern hemisphere, harvest root vegetables in September, in the southern hemisphere harvest in March.

Home-growers have limited space, so for this reason you need to make the most of your plot and nothing supports this maxim better than the idea of continually cropping your leafy and heavy cropping, above-ground crops. Keep picking the produce from the plant to force it to keep producing more flowers for pollination and, thus, more fruits. If you keep picking kale leaves, more leaves will grow, giving you more food; if you keep picking legumes, more will grow in their place. And so on. This is best practice and will extend the food-producing life of the plant and make you happier as a result! The plant does this because it thinks it's been attacked or eaten, as it would naturally, so it produces more potential seeds. You benefit hugely from this natural process.

Occasionally, it's a good idea to leave crops on the plant. If you're attempting to grow a monster pumpkin or you want to collect seeds from your plants, leave a few of the fruits to ripen and grow. This can, and probably will, result in less food than you can eat all at once but it will serve you in the long run as you can harvest a huge bounty (as with the pumpkin) and make yourself self-sufficient in seeds which can very quickly make your endeavours in domestic horticulture near-enough free!

The process of growing that I've discussed in this book – by planting lots of plants that work together – also means that there are plenty of crops to harvest continually and often foods that go well together on the dinner plate, such as courgettes and tomatoes. Following this approach therefore means that you'll have groups of produce to harvest simultaneously rather than just lots of one crop, so you'll be able to make full meals rather than just huge piles of mashed potatoes...

Try to keep this approach to your growing and sowing so you'll have a continual, eclectic supply of edibles coming to fruition at the same time and that complement each other. The frequent annoyance of small-plot growing is that you harvest something but its contribution to the dinner plate is small and underwhelming. This can undermine your efforts and lead to a general apathy towards your fantastic food plot. By growing combinations of vegetables, you'll find that you harvest enough of a few different crops that you can eat together as whole meals, which will buoy your enthusiasm and gain you general kudos from friends and family.

If you accidentally harvest too much of one plant or you pull your root veg too early it's fine, just re-sow and keep going. You'll still enjoy the food and you'll have a good meal from the plant in all likelihood. If you stick to the approach in the planting chapter, continually re-sowing every few weeks, you'll always have a new plant coming into harvest shortly so you'll hardly notice the loss and

you might discover a better taste or way to use the harvested plant.

There is no wrong way of doing things, just learn from each mistake and keep going. One way to avoid this issue is to use the app I mentioned earlier in the book, Koubachi. This app will tell you when you should likely harvest your crops. If you haven't yet set this up, simply download it and calibrate the app (tell it which plants you are growing). Even simpler, set up a reminder on your phone when you sow the seeds, based on the pack information, which will give you a benchmark to work to but remember that there is no rule to when to harvest: with microgreens (seedlings of crops only 4–5cm tall) you can sometimes harvest these only 7 days after sowing. It all depends on what you want to do and when you want to eat them, so don't be afraid to get stuck in and taste them.

Food growing is all about taking your time. In the modern world, everything is hectic, rush and hurry, but you cannot speed up the growing process; it forces you to slow down and enjoy the finer things. Try to treat this as relaxation, a time when you disconnect from your busy life. This is one of many good reasons to embrace growing and it will make the results that much more satisfying.

Growing your own does take some learning, though. It might surprise you at first just how long things take to get going but then suddenly the growth will be exponential and quite swift. A way to deal with this is to follow the book and sow your seeds, then get on with the other tasks. This should keep you busy and focused. What this can do is leave you surprised by the speed at which vegetables grow and thus at which produce is ready for harvest once it has become established. To allow for this, keep space in the freezer for a glut of crops and prepare recipes around the crops you are growing, because the worst thing you can do is waste them. By having eclectic recipes you'll be able to make the most of your plot and not leave produce sitting (and rotting!) in your fridge.

In a nutshell, here's your five-point plan for harvesting

When?

Harvest leafy crops continually but don't take too many leaves or else the plant will die. Root vegetables can be pulled after two months if you want sweet but small crops, otherwise leave them until autumn. Harvest crops collectively if possible so you produce whole-meal portions, not just a little or a lot of just one crop.

Why?

If you keep harvesting you'll keep the plant producing. Harvest in batches to give you more food and make your food go further.

How?

Hold the branch from which the crop is growing and twist; usually if it doesn't release from the branch it's not ready. If you're harvesting when the crop is young and unripe, try not to damage the plant when removing the crop. Ease root veg up with a small fork – pulling it from the top by grabbing the foliage will normally leave the root in the soil and give you a handful of leaves!

What?

Harvesting is the realisation of all your hard work but don't be surprised if it takes the plant time to get going before you can eat the food it produces. Once it is established it will provide frequent bounty!

Last penny's worth...

Plant a combination of fruiting and leafy vegetables to ensure you have a variety of crops coming through continually throughout the season.

Conclusion

This book is merely a guide, instructions for a way to grow, but I know (from experience!) that we're all different and people approach these things differently, so if you don't like our planter or our planting plans – create your own. I'd love to see the results and wish you the best of luck with all your edible endeavours.

This is also true for the materials you use: I've detailed globally available resources but you might know something that works better; success comes from adapting to your environment, so in that way you'll be behaving just like your crops!

Urgency is not something you associate with gardening. The plants simply won't have it. Those with the greatest patience will have the best rewards. You must nurture your garden and it will slowly pay you back. This is the majesty of growing; part of the taste you experience is due to the effort and time you have invested in it. Ask anyone who grows their own food – rainy days spent checking the crops, the careful sowing of each seedling, that is half the taste.

My approach has been to use modern technology to power your growing experience and allow you to fit this into your busy lifestyle. Food growing should be enjoyable, and with measured, precise exertion you can easily manage a small plot. This will enhance the food you put into each meal and get your family experiencing new flavours. I would also suggest using social media to document your progress so that you have a reference point to learn from for next year and can get guidance from others who might be growing locally and with whom you can share personal tips. A relevant, ordered reason for Instagram – who knew?!

This leads nicely into my approach to mistakes. I've made plenty. Wrong crops, wrong time, wrong place. Errors are part of the process, so enjoy them, try to see what caused the problem and adapt your approach for the next time. The best thing about gardening is that there is always another crop you can sow, another plant to grow into the space left by the previous one, another tasty solution that will be ready to eat in a matter of weeks. So get out there and sow the wrong veg, I'm with you the whole way and sometimes the results might be surprisingly rewarding!

It's very important to realise that focus is the best way to get the best results. Don't start lots of different plots and think you can manage all of them at once without help. If this is your first time growing then pick the best spot around your home and stick with that for the first year. Your plot size should grow as your confidence does! However, if you're feeling brave, go ahead and be sure to share the results with us.

It finally comes to end the book. Hopefully you have seen that I merely advocate you taking a stewardship role in the growing process; in a very good way, nature will do pretty much what it wants. You are there to help it when it needs your help and that's it really. This process is as old as the hills and growing in a considered way, where plants work together and everything grows organically, is what has happened for millennia – long before we told crops that they had to grow in rows. All this should serve you to realise that there is no wrong or right way but that you just need to let nature do what it needs to do and provide it with encouragement. If you follow the simple processes I talk about in this book you'll have plenty of food but you'll also learn as you go. You'll see how crops fight and share space and the ingenuity they have for gaining access to light and food. By working with nature you'll also taste flavours and textures you might never have had before; the flavour of beans and peas picked from your garden is something better than you'll get even in the best restaurants, so go forth and sow!

Resources

Garden Organic
www.gardenorganic.org.uk
A wonderful resource for food growing the organic way. Great for advice and they sell lots of different seed varieties so have a look through their catalogue.

Rodale's Organic Life
www.rodalesorganiclife.com
Organic recipes, lots of brilliant tips for creating a more eco lifestyle for yourselves and some really insightful garden know-how.

RHS
www.rhs.org.uk
The bible. The website has had a complete overhaul and is very easy to use to find plant guidance and detailed knowledge of the gardening kind. Look out for events and open gardens.

Gardeners' World
www.gardenersworld.com
Excellent open and approachable resource that gives guidance, recipe hints, and expert suggestions including quick videos.

Connected Roots YouTube
www.youtube.com/ConnectedRootsUK
We've got several videos that show how to find plots around your home, deal with problems and look at working with your plot.

Twitter @ConnectedRoots
The place you can ask questions. I'll deal with growing throughout the season and I'll have videos showing lots of the main points discussed in the book, if you need further clarity.

Facebook
www.facebook.com/connectedroots
This is where I talk about urban gardening in a visual form, bringing through videos you ask me to produce and showing how some of our Connected Roots plots are getting on.

Pinterest
www.pinterest.com/connectedroots3

Koubachi
www.koubachi.com
The brilliant app that can give you timely and relevant crop information set to your location and calibrated to your plot.

***permaculture* magazine**
www.permaculture.co.uk
Where to go for when you really want to grow with nature and do things as organically as possible. Global resources to make use of.

Garden Plan Pro
www.gardenplanpro.com
Great app for android users. Adapts to your location and has all the crop varieties you could ever think of.

Google Keep
www.google.com/keep
Use this app! It will help you plan so you never have to think about your gardening tasks and you can set reminders to location, giving you a nudge when you get home from work!

IFTTT
https://ifttt.com
Recipes but not the kind you're thinking of. Helps you get reminders when it will rain, when it will be sunny and when you take instagram photos.

Index

Acknowledgements

Thank you to **Janelle Conn** for her help and immense guidance in crafting the planting plans and creating some stunning food plots all over London.

I'd like to thank **Fortnum & Mason, Keats Farm, Neil Carlson and Martine Padwell and Matt Cook and Ashleigh Robinson** for their time and patience!

Emma Graham for the intelligence and support in making this book actually possible and mostly legible.

The wider **Connected Roots team** for bearing with my writing absences.

My old man for giving me the love of growing and showing me what to do in the first place!